Fundamentals of Effective Mentorship

In an ever-changing environment, organizations are required to identify and implement numerous decisions about strategy and operational activities. Organizations must consider aspects such as research and development, financial planning, data analytics, information technology, marketing, and production. However, organizational leaders must not neglect the importance of a critical element, which is human resources.

The ability to cultivate the internal capacity and healthy workplace culture can guide an organization to leverage unique abilities, achieve meaningful objectives, and maximize the possibility of sustainable success. As a result, the ability to encourage two-way learning relationships through mentorship can help organizations to improve effectiveness. A mentorship program can empower mentees, mentors, and program leaders to share best practices. The mentorship process is integral for promoting the professional and personal growth of stakeholders within an organization. Through a structured and specifically designed mentorship, the implications of effective mentorship could positively impact individuals, groups, institutions, and broader communities.

Mentorship can occur both formally and informally in diverse areas such as education, business, medicine, law, engineering, technology, arts, sciences, and multi-disciplinary domains. This book communicates recommendations for the facilitation of mentorship programs and development of mentorship relationships based on experiences from a practitioner lens. Readers are reintroduced to mentorship and will learn about the value that can be created for an organization. The exploration of identities, possible outcomes, approaches, and accessibility can spark ideation about recommendations for the reader's organizational context. Readers will embark on a journey to generate new or challenge existing insights through reflective guiding questions.

Figure 1.1   A visual representation of mentorship components. (Developed by Amelia Knop.)

mentors as facilitators. A mindset of facilitative learning encourages individuals to ask open-ended questions, spark reflective practice, and avoid judgment about presented insights. The mentor can share knowledge, skills, and experiences where appropriate, but should seek to promote higher-level thinking from the counterpart through conferencing. A facilitator must determine a balance between illustrating best practices and guiding individuals through a process of self-discovery. As every individual possesses a diverse profile of strengths, improvements, backgrounds, aspirations, or preferences, the relationship identity will emerge specific to the participants. As a result, mentorship evokes a non-linear and iterative process for involved parties to expand learning in an individualized manner. The trajectory of mentorship progress could differ based on relationship factors, interaction activities, and participant identities, so a growth orientation should be fostered.

The mentorship landscape embraces diversity as participants from unique perspectives can share asymmetric information to broaden learner horizons. An understanding of individual needs is central to the design and implementation of programming, so purposeful conversations can illuminate matching or onboarding considerations. As a construct that invites divergent starting points and does not require standardization, adaptability is inherent within mentorship. The activity meets the candidate at the current developmental stage and helps generate the necessary abilities to pursue the next achievement level. A blend of task and relationship behaviors is embedded as exchanges can offer practices for performance and connectivity. A mentor can serve as a bridge to the organizational core as individuals create awareness about values and artifacts. In essence, the mentorship approach captures a dynamic relationship between unique identities with an aspirational focus based primarily on mentee objectives.

Differentiation of Mentorship and Coaching

To position a mentorship construct more precisely, a comparison with organizational and educational terms is conveyed. The coaching construct may initially prompt thinking about an athletic context where designated individuals provide instructions at practices and illustrate tactics at games. However, organizational coaching more broadly leverages the experience of an individual to guide identified members through problem-solving scenarios. A coaching process can support the professional and personal development domains through differentiated learning opportunities. A coach may focus less attention on disseminating advice and alternatively invite participants to engage in decision-making with guiding questions for consideration. A specified coach can use diverse interactional techniques to support the improvement of role-based and soft skills. The pivot between asking questions, processing responses, and engaging in follow-up can motivate members to consolidate best practices for implementation as an ongoing journey of self-discovery. A coaching activity can generate competence and confidence for participating stakeholders, which align with the salient mentorship task and relationship elements.

The mentorship and coaching areas possess synergies as the positions adopt tactful strategies, but clear classifications can situate the approaches separately. First, a coaching environment may distribute feedback with an emphasis on achieving outcomes. The mentorship landscape may delve deeper into the process factors to illustrate unknown or unconsidered views. Second, the coaching scope may be narrower using a lens of development in a specific context with conditions. The mentorship relationship could be more general, with a fostered connection to support multiple learning

Mentorship and Coaching	
Mentorship 👤	Coaching 👥
• Process Orientation	• Outcome Orientation
• General Context	• Specific Context
• Facilitator	• Communicator

Figure 1.2   A comparison of mentorship and coaching. (Developed by Amelia Knop.)

areas. Third, a coach may partake in regular introspection about tactics for communication to ensure common understanding about implementation activities. A mentor can instead share relevant insights to spark thinking as a facilitator for an individualized journey (Figure 1.2).

Differentiation of Mentorship and Teaching

An analysis of the teaching construct is important to recognize the overlap and divergence with mentorship. Teaching represents a process of imparting theoretical knowledge through strategies to support learner acquisition. The transmission of information focuses on mobilizing cognitive resources so that individuals can expand their portfolio of abilities. Although teaching can occur informally, the formal teaching profession requires a prerequisite level of academic training. The educational requirements generate theoretical insights that are needed to convey abstract best practices in understandable terms for the specialized subject matter. A student-centered approach could be adopted, but assessment reporting must adhere to governing associations based on learning goals and curriculum areas. A directive style may be prioritized where the designated expert shares relevant perspectives and seeks confirmatory responses from learners through deliverables. The teaching activities could blend content strategies, such as concepts, examples, and implications, with communication elements in multimodal forms. The teaching conditions are often clearly specified with an audience, location, timeframe, and topic.

As mentorship and teaching both implement learning-oriented interventions, precise clarifications are valuable. First, a teaching context emphasizes achievement of theoretical goals based on established

Mentorship and Teaching	
Mentorship 👤	Teaching 👥
• Application	• Theoretical
• Formative Feedback	• Competency Assessment
• Managed Power Dynamics	• Hierarchical Relationship

Figure 1.3 A comparison of mentorship and teaching. (Developed by Amelia Knop.)

expectations from authority positions. The mentorship domain increases attention to application or practical elements with co-construction based on unique relationship needs. Second, the teacher identifies competency of learning candidates through an assessment process with a computed proficiency score. The mentor instead focuses on feedback exchange without an evaluation score as a formative opportunity for growth. Third, a teaching position naturally cultivates a hierarchical relationship with a power imbalance. The mentor role may involve positional boundaries, but the lack of formal evaluation manages power dynamics (Figure 1.3).

Differentiation of Mentorship and Leadership

An understanding of the leadership construct is necessary to identify similarities and differences with mentorship. Leadership can include the aptitude to impart decision-making for organizational units with consideration for conflicting interests and diverse stakeholders. The leadership approaches could differ based on organizational needs, but individuals are influenced through expressed goals. Leadership is multi-disciplinary, as roles of additional responsibility exist in any hierarchical structure. As individuals transition in a leader pathway to an elevated position of decision-making, a candidate may simultaneously become increasingly distant from the directly impacted stakeholder group. The leadership outlook prompts thinking about how to motivate or influence followers, where objectives originate from an overarching level. The pursuit and achievement of specified targets are critical to organizational progress, so leaders may have a duty to ensure completion in a timely manner. A leader could develop referent power through the nature of

Mentorship and Leadership	
Mentorship	Leadership
• Individual Unit Goals	• Collective Goals
• Facilitate Nurtured Relationships	• Directive with Authority
• Power Balance	• Clearly Separate Roles

Figure 1.4   A comparison of mentorship and leadership. (Developed by Amelia Knop.)

relationships, but positional power automatically emerges through the designation. The leader and mentor can both assume roles in a formal and informal manner.

Although mentorship may be viewed as a subset of leadership, the two constructs exhibit evident distinctions. First, a leadership domain emphasizes goal achievement for nested collectives whereas mentorship focuses on objectives for individual units. The two approaches can be complementary as designates may pursue blended functions in organizational contexts. Second, a leader may need to concurrently inspire and manage organizational members. The managerial lens can appear directive and evoke authority, while mentorship may be facilitative and depend on a nurtured relationship. Third, leadership may more clearly separate roles in an organization such as employer and employee. A mentor and mentee may perceive psychological safety due to the lessened power imbalance, which can spark honest dialogue in the dyad (Figure 1.4).

Mentorship Dichotomy 1: Peer and Traditional Relationships

The articulation of mentorship dichotomies can illustrate relational, program, and organizational unit considerations to guide planning and implementation. The first contrast between peer and traditional relationships investigates the connection between participants. A peer-to-peer relationship represents similarity based on specific identities such as tenure, status, education, age, or discipline. The matchup could originate from overlap in visible and invisible identities, where the participants voluntarily select counterparts or encounter allocations due to expressed data. Although the mentor and mentee candidates may have a high level of similarity, the participants are not identical and could possess complementary alternative identities. The approach may be viewed as contemporary since the reduced power imbalance challenges a past practice of senior–junior connections. For instance, a younger and newer manager could mentor an older and experienced manager about technological infrastructure. An advantage of similarity could be increased comfort to share honest perspectives and enhanced relevance of compiled feedback. A disadvantage could be the absence of generalizable insights from a higher level.

A traditional senior–junior relationship distinctly compartmentalizes participants with designated authority for the senior member and innocence of the junior member. A power difference would be evident in the relationship, which supersedes any salient similarity area and reinforces relative social capital. The unequal position thresholds evoke a higher formality of interactions, but the mentor could serve as an advocate for advancement and mobilize resources with greater simplicity. For example, an executive team member could mentor an aspiring middle manager to build capacity from a system viewpoint. An advantage of the divergence is that the mentor can offer novel perspectives to the mentee in unfamiliar areas and create learning opportunities. A disadvantage is the fear of judgment, which can limit appropriate vulnerability (Figure 1.5).

Peer Relationships   **Traditional Relationships**

Figure 1.5   An overview of relationship types. (Developed by Amelia Knop.)

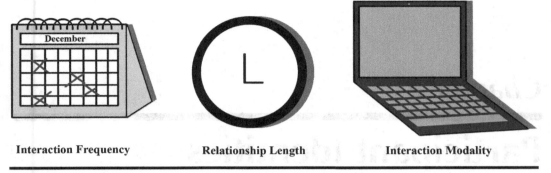

| Interaction Frequency | Relationship Length | Interaction Modality |

Figure 1.6   An overview of program considerations. (Developed by Amelia Knop.)

Consolidation of Mentorship Defined

The recognition of mentorship as a two-way learning relationship for best practice exchange based on collaborative objectives situates the construct in organizational contexts. A practitioner is invited to think critically about views of mentorship in the institution to pinpoint areas of overlap or divergence. Although mentorship can transpire in numerous ways, upcoming content will delve into formal programs with at least one individual unit. The intention is to simulate organizational programs and offer general suggestions for adaptable implementation.

Chapter 2

Participant Identities and Responsibilities

An investigation of resonating factors at the individual or micro level can cultivate conditions for both mentors and mentees to prosper in a developmental relationship. Although participants possess diverse abilities and experiences, commonalities in overarching identities and expectations can offer a general framework. This chapter will capture skills, values, and characteristics to consider for dyadic mentorship relationships, while highlighting possible responsibilities and screening mechanisms. An intention is to explore applicable elements to achieve task and relationship objectives in a meaningful manner. The needs in organizational contexts are unique, so introspection about mentor and mentee profiles is necessary from the program facilitators. An awareness about existing and anticipated skills can guide planning of professional or personal development activities. The co-construction of mentorship positional responsibilities can clarify assumptions and reiterate commitments to mitigate ambiguity for the participants. As relationships can evolve organically over time, the attention to identities or responsibilities serves as the initial baseline and can benefit from consistent review.

The guiding questions illustrate a viewpoint for practitioners across organizational environments to process the specification of program participants. First, individuals should consider: What identities are necessary to enhance intellectual capacity and healthy workplace culture, and why? The identities can represent dynamic constructs that can change through mentorship experiences in formal and informal settings.

DOI: 10.4324/9781032715247-3

An improvement of intellectual capacity suggests that individuals think critically and creatively about strategies for accumulating best practices. The perspective of healthy workplace culture may be supplemented with task-based activities, but the relational element could be emphasized as the primary influence. As a result, recognition about identities can demonstrate overlap or divergence between categories. Second, practitioners should consider: What are the common dynamic or static responsibilities of mentors and mentees within a two-way learning relationship, and why? The responsibilities for distinct roles can determine the expected duty of participants, while engaging in constructive discourse at an early stage can address misconceptions. The dynamic components could adapt regularly and in an interactive manner, but the static elements may display limited change. Although static may be perceived as restrictive or negative in a developmental context, an area of consistency could support norm development in a relationship. Through an overview about possible identities and responsibilities, program coordinators can pinpoint relevant facets of the organizational context.

Enriching Conditions for Mentorship

The outlook for participant identities and responsibilities is to empower individuals to thrive in a learning relationship. An underlying theme is the value of diversity and versatility, as engagement with alternative perspectives and development of new techniques has potential to spark positive change. An intuitive viewpoint may assume that relationships based on similarity are ideal due to the intersecting identities. However, program facilitators have an opportunity to strategically design matchups with diverse elements to initiate two-way learning. The review of program goals and participant aspirations could guide the matchup process. An enriching context focuses on authenticity and psychological safety, where individuals can express perspectives based on truth and comfort. As a result, analysis about identities and responsibilities within orientation sessions or onboarding meetings can evoke reflection from the outset. The learning setting should simultaneously embrace existing abilities and motivate individuals to expand competencies in a living portfolio. The mentorship environment could be aspirational as participants are encouraged to pursue new possibilities. As individuals may not think regularly about deeply held personal elements, a mentorship relationship can activate self-awareness.

Educational Opportunities and Lived Experiences

The skills, values, or characteristics of mentors and mentees can evolve from a combination of educational opportunities and lived experiences. First, educational opportunities can represent formal learning contexts where individuals grow from theoretical programming. An undergraduate degree can impart introductory knowledge across diverse disciplines as the individual completes activities to assemble best practices. A graduate degree can offer autonomy for learners to evaluate societal phenomena and conduct research projects to expand available insights in the scholarly community. A professional certificate could provide specialized topics for individuals to build novel capacity for intervention in institutions. An organizational training workshop or designation could disseminate relevant guidance for operating in any given context and showcase cultural norms. The mentorship relationship can formally convey perspectives to participants through mentor discernment activities, mentee initiation sessions, and program learning deliverables. As a result, mentorship can be a pillar of educational programming.

Second, lived experiences can pinpoint informal or tacit information shared through interactions, activities, or adventures. The personal upbringing, where individuals receive diverse guidance from family members, friends, educators, and supervisors, can either offer perspectives or prompt consideration of a novel philosophy. Any adversity in the developmental journey can challenge individuals to revise taken-for-granted assumptions or reinforce resonating strategies. The broader society can portray implicit expectations based on an aggregation of organizational units, while travel across geographic areas can ignite awareness. The mentorship relationship can informally present aspects for cognitive consideration through conversation and observation. Although individuals have a current profile at the program initiation, a mentorship intervention can simultaneously generate personal understanding through education and experiences (Figure 2.1).

Mentor and Mentee Participant Skills

A specification of possible skills for mentors and mentees can encourage reflection about the existing or prospective abilities. The skills construct is viewed as achievement or proficiency in a particular area. The resonating

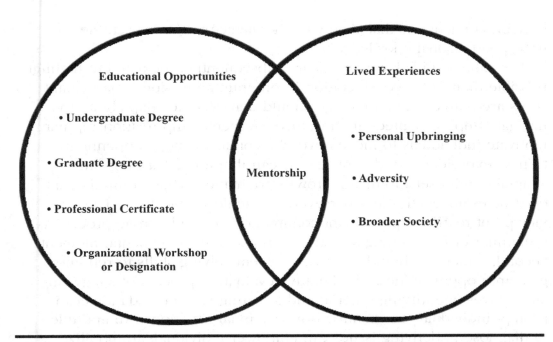

Figure 2.1   A comparison of educational opportunities and lived experiences. (Developed by Amelia Knop.)

skills for mentors are initially considered to identify compelling candidates. First, a mentor should communicate effectively through verbal or written modalities to ensure meaning is conveyed in a sensitive manner. The modality of in-person, virtual, or blended mentorship could influence the prioritization of sub-skills. An in-person program could focus on verbal and non-verbal cues, whereas a virtual initiative could leverage textual elements. If a mentor does not communicate clearly and consistently, the mentee may encounter misunderstandings. Second, a mentor should implement active listening skills to engage in sense-making at a deeper level. Although the mentor may have more experience in a specific context, a mentee-centered relationship leverages narratives from the mentee counterpart. The mentor should participate authentically and attentively within the learning conversation. An interest in expressed mentee viewpoints can permit mentors to reintegrate insights into future dialogue. Third, a mentor should adopt critical and creative thinking skills to encourage mentees to achieve at the highest possible level. The critical approach represents an ongoing willingness to challenge status quo situations for improvement. A creative mindset pinpoints any unique strategies or activities that align with the mentee's needs to activate untapped personal knowledge.

The salient skills for mentees are subsequently articulated to highlight possible themes for consideration in program admission if participant spots are scarce. First, a mentee should demonstrate adaptability to navigate unprecedented circumstances. A mentorship relationship may motivate individuals to move beyond a comfort zone, so openness to new experiences and connections can illuminate learning. An adaptable mindset captures a growth orientation where an individual overcomes adversities and perseveres to achieve objectives. The viewpoint reaffirms participant commitment to the learning process as unfamiliar or challenging scenarios can evoke developmental moments. Second, a mentee should cultivate problem-solving skills to reframe gaps into opportunities. The iterative evaluation process of suggesting alternatives, identifying criteria, and selecting recommendations can prompt individuals to examine organizational situations. An aptitude to diagnose underlying issues can empower individuals to mobilize insights for improved success. Third, a mentee should develop collaboration skills as an interpersonal avenue to foster compelling relationships. The ability to share personal viewpoints and embrace improvement comments should be balanced to expand best practices. Although an individual may accept suggestions from a counterpart, composure to genuinely process feedback and resolve conflict can mitigate relationship disruption. As mentors and mentees could assume roles simultaneously, a blended profile of skills could be adopted from participants (Figure 2.2).

Mentor and Mentee Skills	
Mentor	Mentee
• Communication	• Adaptability
• Active Listening	• Problem-Solving
• Critical and Creative Thinking	• Collaboration

Figure 2.2   An overview of mentor and mentee skills. (Developed by Amelia Knop.)

Mentor and Mentee Participant Values

An examination of pertinent values for mentors and mentees can invite participants to consider priority areas to guide behavior. The value construct is interpreted as the personal beliefs that influence decision-making and sense-making for encountered situations. An overview of mentor values is conveyed initially. First, a mentor should demonstrate honesty throughout the interaction process. The willingness to share constructive feedback or engage in difficult conversations is critical to spark meaningful learning for collaborators. The mentor should think critically about the communication approach to ensure kindness and sensitivity, but courage is necessary to provide relevant insights. The honest dialogue should be bidirectional, as mentors should embrace suggestions from mentees to reinforce two-way learning relationships. Second, a mentor should exhibit respect in every statement and action to create an environment of physical, mental, and emotional safety. Although the intention may be framed positively, an individual may understand a situation uniquely based on divergent heuristics. As a guiding suggestion, a mentor should serve as a role model and behave in a manner that aligns with reciprocated expectations. A respectful disposition must be maintained both within and beyond the role, as broader community members will observe actions across diverse contexts. Third, a mentor should display authenticity with truth to the self and acceptance of personal areas for development. A mentor may be perceived as an all-knowing or ideal individual, but ongoing reflection and acknowledgment of opportunities for growth showcase lifelong learning. The awareness about guiding values and underlying biases can evoke understanding to navigate emerging situations. As the mentor is in a position of responsibility, the representative should capture honesty, respect, and authenticity throughout organizational behaviors and interactions.

The possible values to emphasize for mentees are examined next to compile guiding principles. First, a mentee should possess curiosity to engage in ongoing self-improvement and investigate unfamiliar organizational factors. A thoughtful approach of asking open-ended questions and triangulating data can offer an understanding about challenges. Attention to detail and discipline to avoid immediate judgment can ensure considerable information is absorbed in the process. Intellectual stimulation can stem from the diagnosis of intrinsic and extrinsic motivators,

Mentor and Mentee Values	
Mentor 👥	**Mentee** 👤
• Honesty	• Curiosity
• Respect	• Integrity
• Authenticity	• Professionalism

Figure 2.3   An overview of mentor and mentee values. (Developed by Amelia Knop.)

while interest to accumulate new insights is critical. Second, a mentee should prioritize integrity to cultivate a positive personal reputation as a devoted learner and reflective practitioner. The individual should identify clear objectives and demonstrate accountability for achievement, while conveying a moral compass. An ethical decision-making strategy could be adopted so that mentees can decipher complex information and behave in a responsible manner. Although minor errors or lapses may occur, the individual should commit to high standards and address consequences in learning moments. Third, a mentee should adopt professionalism in interactions, communications, and decisions. The participant can examine the expectations within a specific occupation or industry but should consider appropriateness more generally in any activity. As a communicator, word choice, tone, structure, and body language can support or disrupt an identified message. If an individual has any doubt about anticipated or conducted behavior, dialogue with mentors can be valuable to illustrate considerations. The mobilization of emotional intelligence techniques can complement relational strategies. To enhance pursuit of expressed goals, curiosity, integrity, and professionalism should be viewed as interconnected (Figure 2.3).

Mentor and Mentee Participant Characteristics

An articulation of relevant characteristics for mentors and mentees can influence individuals to pinpoint beneficial dispositions. The characteristics construct is represented as a differentiating factor that could be recognized through personal experience. An exploration of mentor characteristics is initially presented. First, a mentor should illustrate ongoing patience as mentees exhibit unique starting points and need consistent support. As individuals can progress at diverse trajectories, belief in the process can be contagious for the counterpart. The discipline to not generate assumptions and instead ask open-ended questions can collaboratively determine the next steps for improvement. The patient approach connects to emotional awareness, where mentors recognize how to react and converse in specific moments. Second, a mentor should display empathy to understand diverse perspectives of the mentee. The compassion to learn about the professional and personal journey of the mentee can guide the mentor to differentiate developmental opportunities. A mutual appreciation of identities can generate a two-way exchange of best practices, while care for individuality can create comfortable conditions for sharing. The consideration of participant needs and interests can align interventions more effectively with the intended audience. Third, a mentor should convey openness to viewpoints that may differ from personal practices. As individuals may have unique tendencies, receptivity to new insights can spark cognitive reconstruction. The accumulated knowledge can enhance sense-making and decision-making activities, while the mentor can concurrently learn from the mentee. A compelling benefit of participation in mentorship relationships for mentors is construction of new insights, so patience, empathy, and openness can maximize opportunities for growth.

The applicable characteristics for mentees are explained successively to offer conducive conditions for ongoing development. First, a mentee should show appropriate vulnerability to reduce barriers and encourage deeper discussions. A willingness to illustrate emotions, offer insecurities, seek assistance, and proceed authentically are valuable to address resonating needs of the participant. The mentee candidate should extend beyond the comfort zone, while mentor behaviors may enhance or hinder the motivation of mentee sharing. Second, a mentee should embody conscientiousness to model engagement within the learning relationship. The mentee can show initiative, dedication, aspiration, and accountability to complete identified activities. Regular introspection about progress and improvement opportunities can prepare a mentee to achieve the personal potential. Attention to relationship needs can strengthen a connection with individualized insights, while consistency conveys expectations with minimal volatility. Third, a mentee should exhibit enthusiasm to generate a positive and enjoyable learning context. An individual who demonstrates a passion for growth can inspire counterparts to invest time and effort. Although adversities may emerge, an optimistic framing can motivate

Mentor and Mentee Characteristics	
Mentor 👥	**Mentee** 👤
• Patience	• Vulnerability
• Empathy	• Conscientiousness
• Openness	• Enthusiasm

Figure 2.4   An overview of mentor and mentee characteristics. (Developed by Amelia Knop.)

individuals to offer best practices and encourage healthy relationships. As mentees absorb numerous information points during the mentorship journey, vulnerability, conscientiousness, and enthusiasm can empower individuals to exchange deeper thoughts about new lessons learned (Figure 2.4).

Mentor and Mentee Participant Responsibilities

A synthesis of strategic and operational responsibility categories for the mentor and mentee within a mentorship relationship can cultivate a starting point for co-construction. The opportunity to leverage diverse perspectives can pinpoint tailored responsibilities for participants based on salient needs. As individuals may pivot between the roles in a connection, the positions are examined collectively. First, the initiation phase involves offering introductions, specifying objectives, and discussing norms. If roles are formally assigned, a designated mentor could invite the mentee to share professional and personal identities when the individual is comfortable. The decision to first ask the mentee could establish the tone for a mentee-centered relationship where the individual engages in voice behavior. As a mentee may display anxiety in an unfamiliar encounter, the mentor could instead offer to present the background initially. The mentor can frame the opportunity to share as an exemplar for the mentee with guiding prompts to mitigate any implied pressure. After initial links are established, ideation about individual and collective objectives can posit a possible trajectory from the current time. A mentor could prepare for the original onboarding or connection session with sample objectives, questions, and frameworks. The resources could be shared in advance, where possible, to provide time for reflection. The use of tangible materials such as whiteboards, sticky notes, or technological interfaces could generate modalities for brainstorming. Although norms will evolve naturally, an initial exchange is important to accelerate the discernment stage. A conversation where the mentor and mentee express expectations of the self and counterpart can transform implicit assumptions into explicit themes.

Second, scheduling meetings, facilitating activities, and planning experiential learning occurs consistently throughout the relationship with input from both participants. The process for identifying and implementing interaction elements emerges from the initial relationship phase. An openness to analyzing practices can shape the relationship as individuals have unique styles and preferences. The meeting schedule could be developed at the outset based on shared availabilities with consideration for frequency, duration, and modality. An additional approach could be for the mentee to contact the mentor for support when needed if a program does not have formal requirements. Although the technique may offer the perception of increased flexibility for participants, a mentee may not initiate outreach over time, and the relationship could deteriorate. As a result, the specification of minimum meeting thresholds and possibilities for complementary interactions could be a compelling strategy. The activity facilitation could be comprised of constructing session agendas, leveraging necessary resources, or providing content for discussion. A mentee-centered orientation could encourage the mentee to suggest topics and goals for each upcoming session. The mentor may mobilize social capital to compile financial, physical, human, intellectual, or technological resources to support the development of the mentee. The participants could collaboratively assemble materials for the sessions to explore diverse perspectives and enhance development. An experiential learning excursion could occur at the organizational office or in community settings. The ideation could prioritize suggestions from the mentee, while the mentor could use expertise to narrow the final selection. If a mentor has familiarity with the activity procedures, the individual could assume responsibility for execution. However, the mentee could instead organize the event to develop and demonstrate novel learning skills. The importance of communication is consistently reinforced to distribute expectations.

Third, the assessment and reporting of participant achievement could adopt a multilevel strategy. As a relationship progresses and milestones are encountered, the closure stage occurs within the micro-cycle or macro-cycle. The micro-cycle refers to a specific segment within the relationship, while the macro-cycle captures the connection in its entirety. An assessment should include diagnostic, formative, and summative elements to consolidate development at multiple relationship phases. The mentee could be invited to conduct a self-assessment of growth based on co-constructed criteria which can be compared to accumulated data. The mentor can complete an assessment scorecard separately to pinpoint the mentee's strengths and improvements. To spark deeper discussion about progress and next steps, reviews could be compared while differences could be analyzed through open-ended questioning. The mentee could be invited to ask for feedback before an assessment to ensure iterative application of advice. Although the evaluation of goal accomplishment may be viewed as unilateral, the mentor should simultaneously engage in self-assessment, and mentee can offer feedback. The initially designated roles may become more dynamic during the relationship tenure, so an alternating opportunity for guidance is valuable. As mentorship is intended as supportive and facilitative, the emphasis should be on descriptive comments. The reporting could be compiled in a multimodal portfolio, while anecdotal notes are included in a synthesis of lessons learned. The responsibility clusters reaffirm the value of collaborative responsibilities, where counterparts are adaptable and reflective during the process (Figure 2.5).

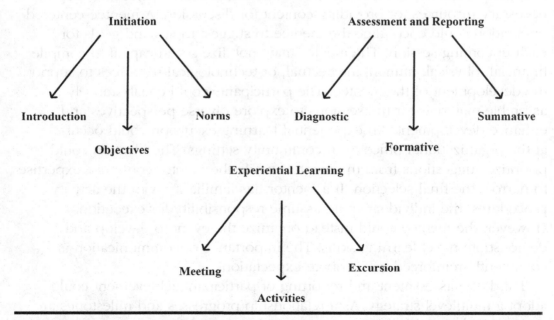

Figure 2.5   An overview of participant responsibility clusters. (Developed by Amelia Knop.)

Identification and Evaluation of Participant Screening Mechanisms

As compelling identities and responsibilities for mentors and mentees are consolidated, an understanding about participant screening can guide acceptance for the program. An idealistic lens suggests any mentor and mentee candidates should have universal accessibility to engage in a mentorship initiative. The opportunity to pursue professional and personal development has the potential to positively impact any individual. However, the reality of resource constraints is that some formalized programs may require strategic admission of participants. First, candidates could be identified consistently based on current organizational roles. For example, all members who joined the organization within the past year could be matched to a mentor. An additional instance could be the connection of managers with a mentor from a higher hierarchical level. An advantage of positional assignments is uniform opportunities for individuals within an identity group. The disadvantage is alternative individuals may need support who are not embedded in the strict acceptance criteria, while mandatory participation could minimize return on investment from lower engagement. A formal preliminary program could be implemented for onboarding to build initial capacity, while optional extension can be permitted for relationships that prosper.

Second, candidates could be selected after voluntarily completing an application process and satisfying organizational criteria. The submission could include a statement of interest and curriculum vitae, while interviews and outreach to referees are subsequently implemented. A professional statement could provide autonomy for candidates to share perspectives in a multimodal manner. The interview can spark deeper dialogue about personalized experiences or values. An advantage is the ability to learn about individual aspirations and motivations to allocate limited resources in a purposeful manner, especially in smaller organizations. The disadvantage is a potential bias in the identification procedure based on reviewer heuristics, while the process can consume time, and individuals may only be admitted at the program's outset (Figure 2.6).

Consolidation of Participant Identities and Responsibilities

The examination of skills, values, and characteristics can illuminate the identities of program participants, while collaborative responsibilities can

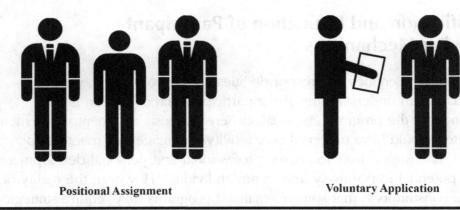

Positional Assignment   **Voluntary Application**

Figure 2.6   An overview of participant identification mechanisms. (Developed by Amelia Knop.)

cultivate an enriching environment. A practitioner is invited to pinpoint necessary identities to encourage achievement in task and relationship domains. The dynamic nature of mentorship connections suggests that individuals should regularly communicate to understand emerging needs. Although relationships will have commonalities, the time and attention to learn about contextual factors can enhance programs. The consideration of participant admission can influence the mentorship scope and activities.

Chapter 3

Signals to Start Mentorship Programs

As organizations may presently implement mentorship activities to a divergent extent, an understanding of signals to spark programming can encourage widespread initiation. The unique organizational contexts are comprised of formal and informal strategies for professional or personal development. However, mentorship interventions have specific distinguishing features from coaching, teaching, and leadership. As a result, an individual in a position of responsibility has an opportunity to advocate for mentorship programs if the structure does not currently exist. Although institutions may already implement mentorship initiatives, introspection about adopted strategies and priorities can revitalize the programming efforts. This chapter will analyze reasons to start or revamp programs based on evident or underlying factors. The investigation of signal types and methodological strategies for data collection can enhance the effectiveness of decision-making. A multimodal approach is necessary to include organizational units from diverse identities. An articulation of recruitment and training elements for designated mentors can impart best practices for implementation and navigate resource constraints. The co-construction of performance indicators can reinforce intellectual capacity and healthy culture objectives, which should be tailored to the resonating needs of the organizational setting. As mentorship is a non-linear learning process, the initiation phase for programs may similarly require adaptability. The willingness to offer a mentorship possibility can serve as a catalyst for organizational change.

DOI: 10.4324/9781032715247-4

The guiding questions encourage practitioners from unique organizational domains to evaluate existing organizational activities and determine how mentorship can address gaps. First, individuals should consider: How does the organization use data collection techniques to identify signals for mentorship program initiation, and why? The longitudinal compilation of quantitative and qualitative organizational metrics is valuable in providing evidence for decision-making. To maximize understanding of organizational patterns and narratives, multimodal streams should be activated to provide a more comprehensive perspective. The resonating themes can pinpoint organizational stakeholder needs, where mentorship can emerge as a compelling solution given the applicability to task and relationship areas. A purposeful pursuit of relevant data sources can illuminate retrospective or prospective challenges for appropriate organizational levels to address in a timely manner. The data collection about mentorship specifically can be complemented with broader organizational phenomena to spark sense-making. Second, practitioners should consider: How can a program achieve specified performance indicators with diverse constraints, and why? The development of mentorship program indicators should process organizational, departmental, and individual needs, so framing of objectives requires considerable reflection. As organizations may operate in environments of emerging complexity, the recognition of resource constraints can guide program scope. The monetary, personnel, knowledge, physical, and technological elements could represent facilitators or barriers depending on the dynamic organizational context. A blend of strategic and operational pillars can influence program design as organizational development activities pivot over time. As a result, an examination about evidence-based signals can prompt program initiation and preliminary design stages based on salient organizational priorities.

Visible and Invisible Reasons to Initiate Programs

An understanding about justifications to start mentorship programs stems from the task and relationship areas, which are highlighted through visible and invisible indicators. First, the task perspective emphasizes the development of intellectual capacity across organizational unit members. The inconsistent achievement of established objectives represents a possible visible signal for mentorship programming. As poor performance may occur due to knowledge, skills, or experiences, a mentorship intervention could facilitate learning about relevant best practices. The decline in productivity or motivation of collaborators and employees in an organizational setting could suggest the need for intellectual stimulation. The individuals may be physically present in the location but are not authentically immersed in the allocated activity. As a result, decision-makers could engage in conversation and observation with stakeholders to extract information about a possible invisible indicator. The expressed concerns about individual competency levels from the self or collaborators could identify diverse organizational needs that require tailored interventions. Although a member may communicate challenges in a clearly visible manner, non-verbalized or less visible issues may still exist. Attention to detail with data collection strategies can uncover hidden elements, while organizational progress can initiate awareness.

Second, the relationship viewpoint prioritizes the cultivation of a healthy workplace culture in alignment with conveyed values or purpose statements. The persistence of destructive conflict can highlight issues about organizational unit connectivity. An argument or altercation could be visible as individuals observe the encounter, but gossip or sabotage could transpire discretely in an invisible manner. An individual must diagnose relationship conflict carefully as respectful constructive discourse can serve as a positive activity for the organization. The recurring nature of stress or pressure within organizational activities could detract from well-being, which can prompt turnover or disengagement over time. A cultivated relationship could invite individuals to honestly express perspectives, whereas superficial connections may not generate comfort to capture authentic thoughts about conditions. Although task performance may be considered primarily, relational aspects can intersect and influence goal achievement. The suboptimal progress in collective environments could imply challenges between participants. An absence of collaboration sessions could simultaneously limit understanding about organizational identity. The abundance of signals can be difficult to pinpoint without diverse evidence compilation (Figure 3.1).

Signal Types to Spark Program Commencement

An introduction to signal categories can provide a model for processing and arranging compiled information from organizational activities. First, the viewing source represents when participants witness behaviors, decisions,

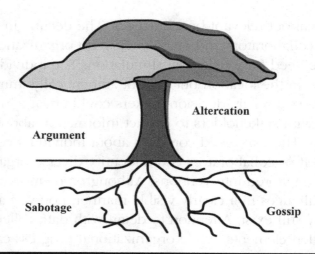

Figure 3.1 An example of visible and invisible indicators. (Developed by Amelia Knop.)

or situations. Individualized heuristics may influence the interpretation of phenomena, so an organization should capture viewpoints from multiple participants. The degree of convergence and divergence can pinpoint recurring trends in an organizational encounter, while concurrently suggesting areas for deeper investigation. The process of viewing activities could occur naturally due to assigned positional responsibilities. For instance, a manager could notice the lack of motivation from the body language of an employee at a debriefing session with a project team. An alternative is spontaneous or unanticipated situations that transpire organically. For example, an individual may interpret the dynamics between individuals who are seated together or separately during a lunch break. Although the viewing could ideally provide significant information, the perceptive environment could generate possible misinterpretation. A decision-maker should delve specifically into the resonating facets, ask open-ended questions to learn about perspectives, and review diverse available data sources.

Second, the interactional source entails when organizational units communicate about unique professional or personal matters. The exchanges between individuals or collectives can offer viewpoints from verbal and non-verbal expressions. A task domain could be evident when an individual asks a colleague or supervisor for guidance about a specific deliverable. The presented insights can generate intellectual capacity as knowledge, skills, and experiences are transmitted across contexts. A relationship realm could be prominent when an individual yells at a counterpart for a disagreement in values or a mistake in performance. The unhealthy conflict could have the possibility to damage an organizational culture based on initial expression and subsequent reactions. An inclination may be to start a mentorship program only when negative interactions are apparent. However, a mentorship initiative could be implemented to elevate the existing high-quality of activities to an expanded level of organizational achievement.

Third, the output source captures the quality of products or services from organizational activities. The lack of achievement in essential areas denotes an immediate need for tailored support to help individuals and collectives enhance performance. An inconsistency in generated returns could similarly illustrate the opportunity for mentorship to facilitate reflection about improvement strategies. A more challenging area to detect is untapped potential when the organizational output is at a reasonably acceptable level. The project participants or supervisors may recognize that greater achievement is possible based on the overarching portfolio of abilities. However, a novel perspective from a mentor who can initiate appropriate dialogue with strategic questions can pinpoint actionable steps for enhanced progress. The output could be viewed as the final generated artifact, such as a report, presentation, or transaction, but a formative process could perceive output as achievement at the end of each stage. The evaluation of performance metrics should be completed with self-reflection mechanisms to leverage unique standpoints. As a result, the consideration of viewing, interactional, and output signal sources can collaboratively uncover priority areas in the organization to justify mentorship programs (Figure 3.2).

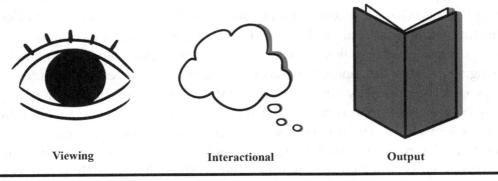

| Viewing | Interactional | Output |

Figure 3.2   An overview of signal types. (Developed by Amelia Knop.)

Multimodal Evidence Collection for Informed Decision-Making

The awareness about reasons and signals to start the development of organizational mentorship programming should be complemented with data collection. Although individuals may have the intuition that a need exists for mentorship, assembly of relevant metrics can be more compelling to seek approval or mobilize resources. The compilation of evidence from multimodal sources in quantitative and qualitative domains can maximize the amount of available information for decisions. A multimodal outlook considers the activation of unique information channels to generate data from a comprehensive representation of stakeholders. The diversification of strategies could mitigate barriers for traditionally marginalized identities through enhanced accessibility to participation. The textual format could involve reading and writing perspectives through words. If written information is collected only, consideration of the audience is critical to anticipate the implications of word choice and structure to generate meaning. The verbal possibility invites participants to share viewpoints through oral strategies, where intonation, pacing, and phrasing can shape the content and delivery of the message. A visual element could include symbols, gestures, movements, and non-verbal body cues, which offer context for the presented insights. As autonomy to participate using any techniques can enhance richness of data, posed questions must be thoughtfully developed to explore pertinent topics.

First, numerical insights for statistical analysis can permit individuals in positions of responsibility to determine differences and relationships among variables. A survey could be prepared to capture perspectives about emerging contextual trends, current organizational phenomena, and mentorship program interests. A balance between general and specific areas could be necessary to position mentorship interventions within the broader institutional and societal landscapes. The survey could ask individuals from diverse positionalities to express agreement to presented statements using a scale or rate concepts based on relative importance. The adopted approach could feasibly generate a larger sample size, but the questions may be less personalized as a uniform instrument is distributed to an entire stakeholder group. The absence of qualitative questions could limit the ability to determine the underlying reasons for selections. An experimental design could be implemented within a mentorship pilot to analyze task or relationship outcomes between program participants and non-participants.

The identification of benefits and drawbacks for participation could guide program administrators about revisions for an official launch. The specification of performance indicators for the individual participants and holistic program could occur through self-report, 360-degree review, or observation activities.

Second, expressed sentiments for thematic analysis can invite organizational coordinators to understand personalized experiences and perceptions at a deeper threshold. An interview could offer environments for individuals to explain organizational challenges and opportunities in an open-ended manner. The supplementary inclusion of questions about mentorship program needs, design, and execution could generate contextual practices for examination. As a tendency may be to prioritize common views, an analyst should explore divergent elements to compile a wider range of possibilities. An anonymized process using transparent confidentiality protocols and independent interviewers could mitigate hesitation about authentic expression. A focus group involving multiple individuals can spark dialogue about resonating situations and offer unique interpretations. The structure should embed rotation for starting the conversation to ensure equitable voice opportunities and reduce dominance from a single person. A record of anecdotal notes could be consolidated to illustrate context about interventions, while archival artifacts may highlight patterns. Although no uniform formula exists for data collection, an organization should blend quantitative and qualitative strategies with diverse multimodal tactics (Figure 3.3).

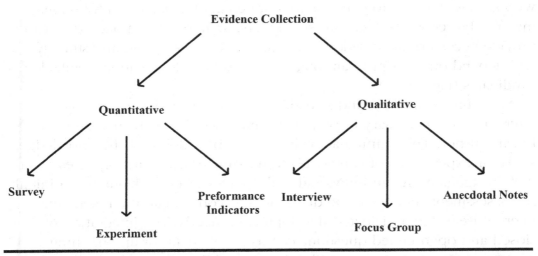

Figure 3.3   An overview of multimodal evidence collection. (Developed by Amelia Knop.)

Mentor Recruitment and Training Techniques

The thoughtful consideration of mentor recruitment strategies is valuable to involve participants with relevant skills, values, and characteristics in a program. First, an application opportunity could be announced and distributed to all possible candidates in an organization or specific identity group. The interested individuals could submit applications and a diverse panel of organizational stakeholders could specify compelling members based on clearly articulated success criteria. The benefit is to encourage any community collaborator to express interest in the mentorship opportunity, while an application process can appropriately screen individuals based on initiative aspirations. A drawback is individuals may be frustrated if an application is compiled and selection is not earned, which could generate concerns about inclusivity. The amount of time to assess applications in a larger context may be significant and detract resources away from the actual mentorship relationships. Second, a recommendation system could be introduced to capture feedback from diverse identities. A supervisor, colleague, or subordinate could have the opportunity to suggest individuals to assume a mentor role within the evolving mentorship program. The multilevel approach to compiling feedback is meaningful as members may observe and converse with candidates through divergent activities. A benefit is endorsement can offer insights about dispositions and effectiveness, while a positive reinforcement culture could be ignited to highlight excellence. A drawback is individuals who are less familiar to collaborators or generate invisible contributions may not be recognized as consistently. The analysis of compiled data can provide necessary information to guide selections. A resonating strategy will depend on clear program objectives and knowledge about available candidates (Figure 3.4).

After the recruitment and selection process concludes, a training intervention is necessary to prepare mentors for the facilitative and non-linear journey. The training activities should be tailored to the knowledge, skills, or experiences of candidates to maximize the return on investment and engagement. As an individual will possess diverse identities, an initial self-assessment survey can be distributed to consolidate the resonating interest areas and anticipated developmental needs. The integration of closed and open-ended questions can assemble data for an enriching discussion about program possibilities. Although training strategies may be unique, common elements could be embedded within initiatives. First, an

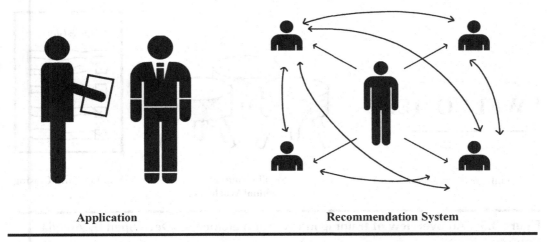

Application   Recommendation System

Figure 3.4   An overview of recruitment strategy processes. (Developed by Amelia Knop.)

onboarding session could be organized collectively to officially welcome mentors to the program and express gratitude. The needs analysis survey could be disseminated in advance so that program coordinators can share themes in the opening discussion. A breakout group format could be adopted to encourage new connections between mentors, where participants can convey expectations, intentions, and salient questions. The collaborative inquiry can cultivate a unified understanding about initiative priorities and resources to build organizational capacity. Second, small group and individual training workshops or modules could be implemented throughout the program term to enhance competences. A blend of in-person and online avenues could be activated based on mentor commitments and preferences. Third, a midpoint and closing survey could illustrate the emerging needs from mentors to guide the next phase of professional development. The captured insights should be stored for review as recommendations could be identified for the next iteration. To launch meaningful training activities, mentors must be actively consulted in the process (Figure 3.5).

Organizational Resource Constraints

An appreciation for resource availabilities and restrictions can guide the initial design of mentorship programs. As challenges may appear

| **WELCOME!** | **Small Group and** | **Midpoint and Closing** |
| Onboarding Session | Individual Workshop | Survey |

Figure 3.5 An overview of training intervention elements. (Developed by Amelia Knop.)

in an organizational environment, program facilitators should think critically and creatively about how to navigate the situation. Although an abundance of resources could offer expanded opportunities for participants, strategic allocation of limited materials may generate improved program success. Financial resources represent monetary amounts or assembled assets that could be embedded within an initiative. A possible misconception is that only private corporations can generate revenue, but the actuality is any organization including non-for-profit environments must leverage some monetary sources. The financial capacity for mentorship programs could stem from budgets, fundraising, sponsorships, grants, or donations. An organization may decide to allocate money for participant honorariums, subsidized experiential activities, or alternative resources to facilitate professional development goals. The opportunity to pursue funding from external agencies or stakeholders could generate an increased ability to design and execute impactful learning interventions. If an institution encounters financial issues, decision-makers may reduce the scope of mentorship programs. As a result, advocates should compile evidence to display contextual improvements from mentorship such as productivity, goal achievement, competitive advantage, and healthy culture. A pilot program could be suggested to investigate the effectiveness of mentorship based on pinpointed organizational signals. As organizations operate in evolving contexts, financial allocations can depend on the effectiveness of interested individuals to showcase task and relationship benefits.

After understanding the financial conditions within an organization or industry, program coordinators can explore four interconnected resource categories in greater depth. First, human resources is an essential element within a mentorship relationship. The value of mentor and mentee time must be considered to ensure enriching opportunities to extend capacity. An organization must identify relevant supporting specialists such as program facilitators, workshop speakers, data analysts, and administrators. Second, intellectual resources can be generated through two-way learning exchanges across organizational units. An awareness about participant identities, needs, and aspirations can emphasize relevant areas in programming. Third, physical resources establish the developmental environment through both the location and available tools. The infrastructure denotes the facilities and configurations for interactions to transpire, while equipment, visual aids, and expressive mechanisms depend on materials. Fourth, technological resources capture the hardware and software necessary to transform insights into outputs. The presence of devices and applications can synthesize information in an unprecedented manner. An evaluation of assets can anticipate pathways for participants to achieve co-constructed goals (Figure 3.6).

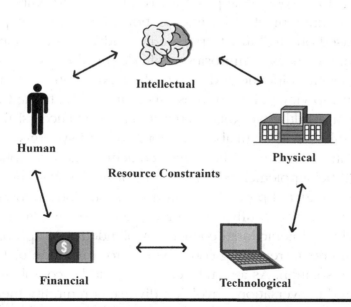

Figure 3.6 An overview of organizational resource constraints. (Developed by Amelia Knop.)

Key Performance Indicators for Task and Relationship Success

The framing of task and relationship elements to conceptualize success is an applicable topic for initial program proposals to decision-makers. The task perspective delves deeper into possible indicators for recognition of improvements in intellectual capacity. First, the achievement of established objectives for individual and collective organizational units can demonstrate program success. A compelling goal should be positioned at an appropriately high developmental level that extends beyond current abilities. The consolidation of longitudinal metrics to pinpoint progress can illustrate the direct and indirect implications of programming interventions. Second, the acquisition of knowledge, skills, and experiences can exhibit abilities to support organizational strategy or operation domains. A showcase opportunity could be organized where mentors and mentees share best practices from the relationship to offer insights to broader community members. A link to institutional values and statements can present the relevance of cultivated elements. Third, the insightful launch of new programs could exhibit mobilization of suggested ideas. A thorough decision-making framework may be adopted to guide the evaluation of possibilities, while participants could be recognized for innovative practices. The intention is to encourage appropriate risk-taking and empower individuals to assume initiative for interventions. Fourth, development could be assessed based on eligibility to pursue new advancement opportunities. A review of competences from positions of additional responsibility could cultivate a leadership pipeline and inspire the next iteration of mentors.

The relationship viewpoint explores salient indicators to capture enhancements in healthy workplace culture. First, the successful completion of team deliverables with equitable contributions and synergistic activities can depict positive dynamics. The perceived achievement in collective projects should be supplemented with feedback from collaborators to learn about conducted processes. Second, a reduction in observed and reported destructive conflicts or human resource complaints could convey positivity in interactional contexts. A blended data approach is critical as less frequent reporting could be due to frustration or lack of confidence in resolution. As a result, reports should be complemented with observations and conversations involving diverse community members. Third, attendance patterns from participants could highlight motivation to engage in institutional activities. As members may be present but not authentically immersed in organizational processes, attendance should be considered with performance. Involvement in team-building opportunities, extra-curricular activity programs, and voluntary professional development initiatives could denote attendance more effectively. Fourth, surveys about well-being metrics such as organizational satisfaction, commitment, motivation, and connection to collaborators could offer information for analysis. An anonymized approach is valuable to invite honest perspectives in the process, while suggestions can be articulated in multimodal terms. Fifth, organizational attrition could be monitored in exit interviews to determine if individuals are departing due to workplace culture factors. A comparison of indicator metrics could occur between mentorship participants and non-participants to pinpoint program implications.

Consolidation of Signals to Start Mentorship Programs

An investigation of the rationale for initiating a mentorship program highlights that visible and invisible factors could influence organizational phenomena. The purposeful mobilization of data collection techniques can assemble insights for sense-making and intervention design. A recruitment and training process must be differentiated based on participant identities, while the recognition of resources can guide facilitators to pinpoint compelling success strategies. A clear articulation of task and relationship indicators could gauge organizational ramifications in a pilot program. A thoughtful plan can be more impactful to generate buy-in from decision-makers.

Chapter 4

Outcomes for Mentees, Mentors, and Communities

As organizations proceed with the initiation of mentorship programs, consideration about possible outcomes can influence decision-making at a coordination level. Although mentorship interventions can generate positive implications in an organizational unit, a simultaneous chance exists that negative ramifications may transpire. This chapter explores resonating outcomes that can enhance awareness during the sense-making process and help pinpoint appropriate next steps for program revisions. A mentorship relationship requires time to achieve potential based on introspection and constructive dialogue. As a result, a similar approach should be applied to a mentorship program at an overarching level. An objective is to spark thinking about consequence types for mentorship initiatives, which can increase or decrease in importance across and within organizational environments. An appreciation for the multilevel context is necessary to specify the convergence or divergence of outcomes for stakeholder identities. An overview of benefits and drawbacks is illustrated as a starting point for analysis, while mitigation strategies are suggested to proactively address challenges. The activation of checkpoints for individuals, teams, institutions, and communities could be valuable to support iterative and ongoing improvement processes. A recognition of discourse and developmental zone alignment can ensure mentorship program structures converge appropriately with organizational needs. The identification of any influencing factors could accentuate facilitators or barriers in a mentorship realm. To maximize the mentorship program impact, coordinators must leverage positives and address negatives.

DOI: 10.4324/9781032715247-5

The guiding questions motivate practitioners from any learning landscape to evaluate expected and unanticipated outcomes in an organizational intervention. First, individuals should consider: How can organizations navigate any complexities effectively, and why? An element of complexity may be perceived with a negative connotation, as difficulties can evoke disruption based on initial plans. However, complexity can concurrently challenge decision-makers to pursue higher standards for mentorship initiatives. If program activities are too simplistic, then the positive implications may not be grasped with as much gratitude. The navigation approach is critical as participants must collaboratively specify and execute strategies to reframe challenges into ideal circumstances. An understanding about the significance or underlying justification for success and difficulty is vital to process contextual factors. The successful approaches in one organizational unit may not necessarily replicate achievement in an alternative landscape despite views about similarity. Second, practitioners should consider: What benefits could spark mentee participation, and why? The articulation of positive program implications can encourage interest from candidates to embark on a mentorship journey. Although some individuals may display an immediate motivation to engage in the learning initiative, counterparts may perceive the program as an unnecessary and time-consuming endeavor. The purposeful collection of data can offer success stories to share with the broader community, while illustrating best practices for future relationship improvement. The authenticity of disseminated experiences can resonate with diverse organizational stakeholders and generate stimulation for prospective registration. A program culture should be grounded in honesty and aspiration as a dynamic ecosystem for development. As a result, speculation for outcomes can guide program pillars in the design phase.

Consequence Types in Mentorship Programs

To simplify the analysis process for mentorship initiative implications, a description of the consequence types can provide a general model for organizing thoughts. First, a positive outcome can help the organizational unit to achieve task and relationship objectives in either an intended or unanticipated manner. For instance, a supportive task outcome could be newly generated knowledge, skills, and experiences to improve the quality of work performance. An ideal relationship outcome could be the cultivation of connections across departments to promote collaboration and novel insight exchange. Second, a negative outcome can reinforce limitations to prevent the accomplishment of participant goals and prompt disruption that opposes intended trajectories. For example, a task outcome could be the contagious distribution of mentor biases or assumptions in areas of exclusivity and inequity to impressionable mentees. A relationship outcome could be a lack of confidence to share new ideas if the mentor creates an environment of pressure or unacceptance. The combination of positive and negative outcomes could uniquely impact organizational members. An individual unit could encounter positive and negative areas, positive elements only, or negative elements only. The benefits for one organizational unit could possibly cause drawbacks or generate additional advantages for another member, so alignment of mentorship relationships within the overall program is valuable to maximize collective gains.

The explanation of implication extremities can be complemented with two additional categories involving blended aspects. Third, a neutral outcome can represent the indifference or absence of effects from a positive and negative standpoint. For instance, a new relationship with an individual in another organization in a cross-institutional program could be neutral for advancement endorsement in the current context. The mentee may build new capacity through the connection, but the mentor may not be positioned to advocate for or against the mentee with organizational credibility. The neutral implication can be challenging to decipher as situations are multifaceted, so a learning exchange could likely have at least some positive or negative element. Fourth, an ambivalent outcome possesses both positive and negative components at the same time. For example, a mentee who is guided to work more independently may increase productivity but demonstrate less inclination to engage in organizational interaction activities. An equivocal situation can emerge from the heuristics of an organizational unit, as ambivalence may occur from a program coordinator position, but not necessarily from the standpoint of an individual member. The positivity and negativity may not be balanced, so attention to relevant data for the phenomena can assist with speculating the relative weightings. The categorization of outcomes may appear straightforward, but organizational situations include countless factors. As a result, the outcome identification could involve complications and evolution over time (Figure 4.1).

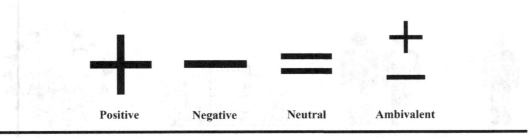

Figure 4.1   An overview of consequence types. (Developed by Amelia Knop.)

Multilevel Perspectives in Mentorship Environments

An investigation of outcomes throughout the diverse organizational levels is important to ensure consequences for unique stakeholders are appropriately considered. First, the individual is denoted as a single person in an institution or relationship. A positive outcome could be higher achievement on a performance evaluation due to developed competences from the mentorship exchange. A negative outcome could be lower confidence and subsequent disengagement due to the interpretation of provided feedback from an assigned mentor. Second, the team is represented as a smaller group involving individuals with a shared identity. A smaller marketing department with a few members could be viewed as a team, while larger departments may instead have sub-committees or project groups to optimize team functionality. A positive outcome could be the cultivated culture for knowledge exchange where members recognize specialty areas and leverage expertise for organizational improvement. A negative outcome could be performance that does not meet or exceed the sum of individual parts due to collaboration conflict. Third, an institution serves as a structured organizational unit that includes individuals and teams. A post-secondary school, accounting office, or hospital could be institutions. The units may be members within a broader organizational system, such as a school board, firm, or ministry respectively. A positive outcome could be improved profitability due to member engagement or productivity. A negative outcome could be lack of organizational alignment with the vision when the many sub-units function in a primarily independent manner. Fourth, communities consist of numerous individuals, teams, and institutions which can intersect to spark phenomena. Outcomes may be tougher to attribute at the broader level, but small acts can collectively generate impact (Figure 4.2).

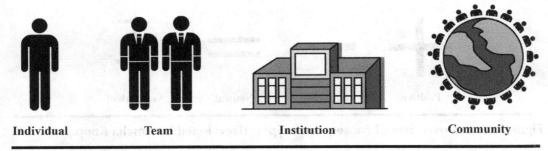

| Individual | Team | Institution | Community |

Figure 4.2   An overview of organizational levels. (Developed by Amelia Knop.)

Mentorship Program Benefits

The synthesis of mentorship benefits for mentees, mentors, and communities can illustrate the value of implemented interventions for diverse stakeholders. The mentee identity is explored initially to pinpoint the implications of two-way best practice exchanges. First, a mentee can develop unprecedented relationships with individuals across organizational units to mobilize knowledge, skills, and experiences. The new interactions can generate lifelong connections with individuals from unique backgrounds, which can extend the current portfolio of professional and personal insights. The opportunity to converse with individuals at higher organizational levels, unfamiliar peers in alternative departments, and newer members with diverse abilities can cultivate capacity. Second, a mentee can demonstrate enhanced self-belief to achieve more challenging objectives from task and relationship domains. The encouragement, support, and tailored guidance from counterparts can activate awareness about strengths or development areas. A mentee-centered relationship could blend cognitive and emotional aspects to expand confidence, realization, and positive identity. Third, a mentee can improve the ability to develop and pursue meaningful goals for individual growth. The constructive discourse can illuminate values and priorities for the learning-oriented member, while establishing action plans for achievement. The identification of smaller milestones within larger ambitious goals can support individuals to navigate a growth journey and designate success strategies for the future.

The mentor stakeholder group is examined next to recognize ramifications of effective facilitation within the mentorship relationship. Although practitioners may believe that benefits in connections resonate primarily with the mentees, the mentors can simultaneously encounter positive elements and possibly to an even greater extent. First, a mentor can refine verbal and written communication tendencies through interactions with a new individual. The mentor may possess significant knowledge, skills, or experiences, but the individual must think critically and creatively to disseminate insights in an understandable manner. An awareness about mentee identities, needs, and preferences can guide the communication tactics with consideration for multimodal avenues. As best practice exchange depends on the transfer of information, the mentor can learn about techniques to converse with diverse individuals. Second, a mentor can enhance introspection abilities as a reflective practitioner. The openness to new perspectives can pinpoint relevant intellectual resources for implementation in organizational activities. An ongoing collaboration between mentorship units can evoke deeper knowledge about values and philosophies to impart positive community impact. Third, a mentor could identify talented individuals for new positions or opportunities through scouting in mentorship relationships. An initiated connection across hierarchical levels can provide insights about developmental activities that could be implemented for prospective members. The distinguished individuals could be recommended for additional responsibility to improve team and organizational achievement. Fourth, a mentor can pursue self-actualization through the willingness to reinvest time and effort into the broader community. The possibility to share viewpoints in a bidirectional manner can provide fulfillment, especially if the mentor is in a static or routine position for a longer period. The mentor benefits signify that the role can be vocational and challenge existing practices.

The broader community is finally explored to showcase the collective consequences for multiple and diverse stakeholder groups. First, a mentorship intervention can spark a culture of lifelong learning as a living forum for best practice exchange. The growth orientation can engage individuals, teams, and organizations across the system to participate in collaborative inquiry. An appreciation for presented perspectives can suggest pivots to strategic and operational pillars. A commitment to creating knowledge can position the organization with a competitive advantage, given the willingness to adapt to evolving phenomena. Second, the community can demonstrate an improved understanding of diversity, equity, and inclusivity. A series of cultivated relationships can highlight unique visible and invisible identities, which can guide decisions to enhance representation in collective activities. Active listening to alternative perceptions can denote developmental barriers and invite stakeholders to revamp taken-for-granted practices. The reflection about organizational

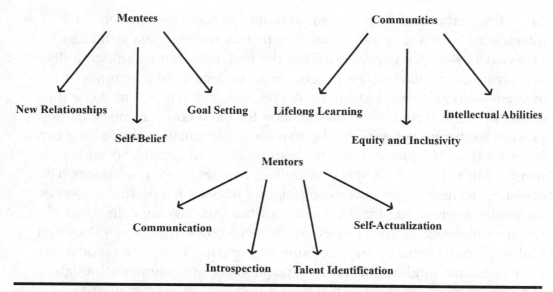

Figure 4.3 An overview of mentorship program benefits. (Developed by Amelia Knop.)

experiences can evoke recommendations to promote authentic belongingness. An institutional environment that encourages uniqueness and permits individuals to integrate identities has the possibility to expand capacity to unanticipated levels. Third, mentorship can generate necessary intellectual abilities from an internal origin in a context with unpredictable constraints. Although organizations may not have the financial flexibility to introduce additional members, best practices could influence engagement, productivity, and creativity for extended achievement. As a result, the benefits for mentors, mentees, and communities can align with both intellectual capacity and healthy workplace culture areas (Figure 4.3).

Mentorship Program Drawbacks

The compilation of program drawbacks for mentees, mentors, and communities can provide context about possible challenges and spark thinking about mitigation plans. The mentee position is investigated originally as relationships can be centered around the stakeholder identity. First, a lack of interest or motivation for the mentee to participate in a relationship can minimize the task and relationship outcomes. If involvement in a mentorship initiative is a requirement of organizational onboarding or advancement, some mentees may not sustain the effort to generate aspirational outcomes from a coordinator standpoint. A perception may emerge that mandatory programs should be removed from the organizational portfolio, but disengagement has the possibility to similarly transpire in a voluntary initiative. The absence of interest could limit the relationship from achieving the intended potential. Second, ineffective feedback or inconsistent guidance could cause mentee confusion about next steps and organizational expectations. If suggestions are unclear or too general, the individual may be conflicted about how to mobilize the co-constructed strategy. The internal turmoil could spark frustration or reduce confidence about decision-making. If the mentor shares perspectives that represent misalignment with the broader organization, the mentee may proceed in a divergent pathway. As a result, the behavior may not appropriately support performance or workplace culture. Third, the inability to establish norms or aspirations for the relationship can delay progress and impart anxiety for the mentee. The imposition of standards or objectives from a mentor can constrain the learning activities, as the mentee may not feel valued in the process. The mentee voice behaviors and collaborative activities are critical to ensure relationship progress in a productive trajectory overall.

The mentor position is presented subsequently to capture challenges from ineffective facilitation or unproductive relationships. First, matchups that are not purposefully created can limit the ability to provide tailored support and may influence future program participation. The assignment of a mentor to a mentee must be thoughtfully considered to ensure appropriate connections based on initiative objectives and participant identities. If the mentor does not have prerequisite knowledge, skills, or experiences, the individual may not feel confident to activate growth from the counterpart. The lack of interpreted benefit for the participants may reduce the motivation to support future mentorship relationships as mentors may perceive minimal impact. Second, an unstructured mentorship intervention could overwhelm the mentor from resource domains. If a program does not provide overarching goals, stages, and materials, the mentor may become emotionally frustrated and view the responsibility as a burden. The increased investment of time and effort into the relationship could result in trade-offs for alternative responsibilities. As challenges compile and the mentor thinks the relationship drawbacks outweigh the benefits, the individual may demonstrate lower engagement to support the mentee. Third, the neglect for mentor training and ongoing program support can shape the potential to spark positive impact. If a mentor feels unprepared and unassisted, the ability to achieve objectives could be diminished. The mentor may achieve a weaker performance than anticipated and lose confidence about how to facilitate learning. Although mentors may be classified as area experts, the participants still require individualized consideration to cultivate a positive developmental experience.

The broader community is analyzed ultimately to demonstrate the interconnected effects of mentorship relationships for diverse stakeholders. First, a program that is not differentiated to organizational priority areas could spark unideal outcomes over time. An initiative may seek to generally build intellectual capacity, but the lack of specificity may invite participants to pursue learning in less applicable areas. Although a learning moment can possess at least some professional or personal benefits, the strategic clarity is necessary to maximize organizational return on investment. Second, an initiative without proper support from organizational decision-makers can pose lost learning opportunities. If a united effort is not displayed, specialists from diverse organizational roles or relevant resources may not be involved. The absence of guidance can perpetuate existing biases or assumptions through reinforced mentorship activities. Third, the assembly of data with low reliability or validity can disrupt sense-making. A single modality for feedback compilation can minimize diversity of perspectives, while irrelevant techniques can offer incorrect details. An acknowledgment of challenges can illuminate mitigation strategies (Figure 4.4).

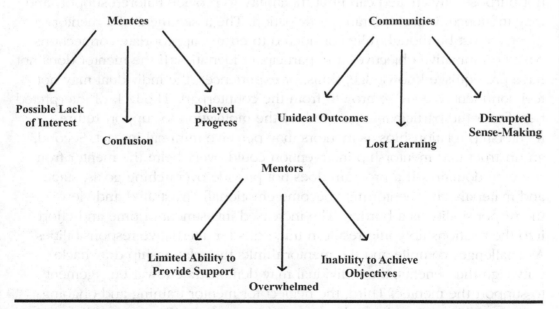

Figure 4.4   An overview of mentorship program drawbacks. (Developed by Amelia Knop.)

Mitigation Plans for Mentorship Program Challenges

The evident difficulties within mentorship relationships and programs can be reframed through compelling mitigation approaches. The mentee, mentor, and community drawbacks can overlap, so strategies could be considered collectively instead of in an isolated manner. First, an application process for voluntary initiatives should involve a statement of interest to understand the intentions of candidates. If a program is required in an organization, an outline of possible benefits and rationale for implementation can generate shared understanding for participants. The screening activities can provide valuable perspectives to determine the appropriate development zone for established connections. Second, overall program expectations should be communicated to mentors and mentees based on organizational values or aspirations. The distribution of institutional resources, feedback models, and guiding questions can provide a general starting point. The organization should encourage differentiation based on needs, but an initial structure can provide overarching clarity. The ongoing checkpoints can stem from co-constructed program standards, which emphasize progress to achieve aspirations. Third, a strategy should be proposed, discussed, and revised about specifications for matchups. A review of program goals, participant identities, and mentorship dichotomies can spark thinking, while input from unique community stakeholders can ensure inclusivity. The iterative approach can facilitate ideation about possible challenges in a proactive timeframe to establish a foundation for initial program success.

An exposition about additional mitigation plans after the program initiation can ensure positive progress. Fourth, training workshops or modules should be designed for mentors consistently throughout the program tenure. The communication about available organizational resources, breakout sessions to offer best practices, and tailored content in interest areas could be integrated. The program should function at the intersection of individual and collective identities to cultivate synergy for task or relationship outcomes. Fifth, the activation of multimodal data collection avenues with quantitative and qualitative methodology should be leveraged. The inclusion of surveys, interviews, focus groups, observations, and archives can consolidate comprehensive information to enhance decision-making. The insights shared from diverse stakeholder positionalities can illustrate possibilities for program design and development. Sixth, program graduates can be invited to discuss experiences for subsequent initiative iterations. An honest conversation can extract considerations for

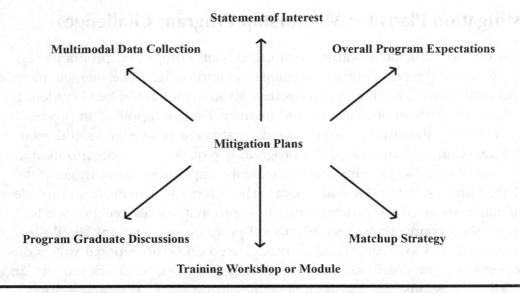

Figure 4.5 An overview of mitigation plans. (Developed by Amelia Knop.)

both mentors and mentees during the discernment phase. A best practices showcase could be organized at the program conclusion to transfer implicit lessons learned to explicit artifacts for prospective participant reference. A mitigation strategy for program risks can possibly address anticipated intervention domains, but consistent, constructive discourse and adaptation are necessary to resolve emerging challenges (Figure 4.5).

Mentorship Program Mediators and Moderators

The ideation about possible mediators and moderators can ignite thinking about factors within the mentorship relationship. A mediator variable can provide an understanding about the link between independent and dependent elements. The suggested scenarios integrate participation in a mentorship relationship as the common predictor, while cultivation of intellectual capacity and healthy workplace culture serve as the outcomes. First, the development of relevant knowledge, skills, or experiences could mediate the connection. The effective or ineffective facilitation of learning about applicable insights, competences, and reference points can influence success. Second, the identified mentorship dichotomy constructs could mediate the link. For instance, a peer relationship may provide comfort for participants to authentically reflect and develop new abilities to achieve task goals. Third, outlined program considerations may mediate a connection. For example, a longer relationship could provide more opportunities to exchange insights and co-construct strategies for fostering a positive organizational culture. Fourth, constructive dialogue could mediate the link through authentic opportunities to uncover assumptions and biases. The personalized experience can facilitate required learning to satisfy initiative goals. Fifth, an environment of psychological safety could mediate the connection. The perceived comfort to share honest ideas can support achievement of professional or personal growth priority areas.

A moderator variable can influence the strength or direction of a link between predictor and result components in a mentorship program. First, a positive or negative individual attitude could moderate the connection. If a mentor or mentee displays a growth mindset in a learning relationship, receptivity to new opportunities could lead to positive outcomes. Second, the alignment of goals or activities to the developmental zone may moderate the link. Appropriate experiences can spark growth for the participant without boredom or unhealthy anxiety. Third, mentor team diversity could moderate the connection. A unique pool of mentors may offer additional insights for sense-making, whereas a homogenous mentor group could reinforce existing practices. Fourth, institutional support could moderate the link through endorsement and materials. If a decision-maker allocates financial, technological, or human resources, experiential opportunities could expand (Figure 4.6).

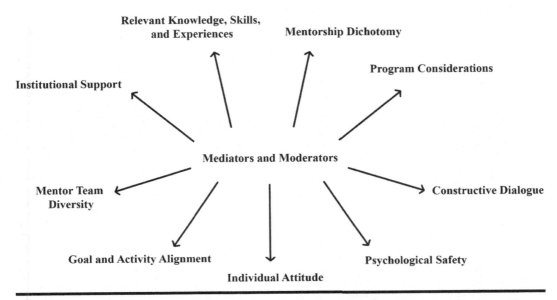

Figure 4.6   A sample of mediators and moderators. (Developed by Amelia Knop.)

Consolidation of Outcomes for Mentors, Mentees, and Communities

An exploration about positive and negative implications for mentorship programs can influence relationship participants to identify compelling strategies. A mitigation plan must be tailored to the contextual environment, while awareness about stakeholder identities can ensure appropriate alignment. The recognition of predictor, outcome, mediator, and moderator variables can prompt thinking about relationship or program activities. An adaptability to address any unprecedented challenges can pivot situations into a positive learning space. A clear awareness about intended outcomes can influence the selection of mentorship styles or philosophies.

Chapter 5

Mentorship Styles and Philosophies

As participants in a mentorship program possess diverse identities and trajectories, an awareness about individualized tendencies can influence learning interactions. Although stakeholders may perceive that specific approaches are most effective, the impact can change based on the organizational environment. This chapter investigates the possible mentorship styles and philosophies that can be adopted from the mentor and mentee positionalities. Through the participation of individuals in a non-linear learning journey, implemented techniques may evolve based on new knowledge, skills, and experiences. The facilitative dialogue may prompt critical and creative thinking about existing mentorship practices. An ongoing conversation about objectives and progress can spark the realization about underlying assumptions. The co-construction of reflection questions to guide constructive discourse can illustrate novel themes for enhanced professional and personal success. The ability to clearly articulate a mentorship philosophy can generate shared understanding about the current sense-making strategies of a given collaborator. An identification of transformational and transactional techniques could highlight implications for task and relationship behaviors. As the willingness to express honest perceptions requires vulnerability, the cultivation of psychological safety within a connection is critical. The strategy to transform implicit viewpoints into explicit best practices can prompt recognition of individual needs. As participating organizational units may have diverse decision-making priorities and

DOI: 10.4324/9781032715247-6

interpretative lenses, each mentorship relationship is unique and necessitates attention to detail.

The guiding questions challenge practitioners from the organizational ecosystem to pinpoint leveraged styles and philosophies. First, individuals should consider: How can the development of a philosophy generate shared understanding, and why? The developmental element reinforces that philosophies can change across temporal horizons. The experiences within the organizational setting can be complemented with interactions throughout the broader community. A philosophical orientation could influence a mentor through presented guidance in facilitative sessions or as a mentee through processing of best practices. The shared component recognizes that mentorship can represent a constructivist process where collaboration evokes unprecedented learning. A willingness to ponder about the participant journeys can capture the motivational factors for selected approaches with compelling rationale. A multimodal strategy could be valuable to disseminate resonating philosophical pillars in an engaging manner for diverse audiences. Second, practitioners should consider: What mentorship styles or blends resonate with a particular philosophy, and why? The specification of mentorship behaviors to facilitate best practice exchange can compile meaningful approaches for participants. Although styles may be compartmentalized into distinct silos, a blended or intersecting profile may align more precisely with specialized programming needs. As initiative participants interact regularly with diverse individuals, a blended style could emerge based on resonating skills, values, and characteristics through exposure to community members. The alignment of style and philosophy is critical for synergy in mentorship activities while progressing toward co-constructed goals. A style that achieves objectives in one context may lead to divergent success in another landscape, so open-ended questioning can challenge individuals to refine an approach based on experience.

Individualized Mentorship Philosophy

The multimodal articulation of a mentorship statement to guide relationship activities can offer insights from a personal perspective. A multimodal design provides options for the program participants to convey thoughts using numerous avenues. The opportunity for expression can expand the richness of presented philosophical pillars, while encouraging metacognition for community collaborators. A mentorship philosophy is important for both the author and counterpart as a baseline for the learning relationship. As a result, a multimodal illustration can permit creators to synthesize themes in a differentiated framework. First, the textual aspect could encompass language selection, sentence structure, and paragraph framing through reading and writing stages. The words can generate diverse meanings based on the sense-making context, so the ability to communicate in a purposeful manner can spark perspective-taking. Second, the visual aspect mobilizes the sense of sight to interpret insights through colors, designs, images, and videos. The activation of visual techniques can emphasize sentiments through explicit or implicit avenues. Third, the auditory aspect leverages the sense of hearing to capture ideas through intonation, pacing, and word choice. The aggregation of sounds can offer both thoughts and emotions in an expression process. A specific combination of multimodal tactics is not required to develop a philosophy, but participants should have autonomy to showcase views (Figure 5.1).

A model for developing mentorship philosophy components should be general enough to provide overall form, while not constraining the ideation process. First, a who element reminds individuals to think about participants. The professional and personal mentors from past formal or informal experiences may guide the current philosophy. Second, a what element encourages members to pinpoint learning objectives, strategies, and identities. The content of programs can influence adopted behaviors and activities for expanded best practices. Third, a when element pinpoints the timeframe for mentorship progress. A specification of forthcoming horizons can clarify the urgency and sequencing of milestones. Fourth, a where element captures the location for mentorship interactions. The environment could extend beyond the organizational landscape if a

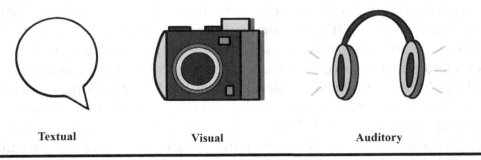

| Textual | Visual | Auditory |

Figure 5.1   An overview of multimodal design elements. (Developed by Amelia Knop.)

participant is open to cross-contextual learning. Fifth, a why element challenges members to convey the reasoning for participation. An awareness about skills, values, and characteristics from both strength and improvement areas can tailor programming. Sixth, a how element invites a tentative presentation of anticipated pathways to pursue novel competences. The recognition about possible learning opportunities can suggest relevant experiences and modalities during the developmental adventure. An initial mentorship philosophy artifact can provide a baseline for conversation in orientation sessions, while organizations may pose questions about the topic for a statement of interest in applications. The mentor and mentee participants could annotate the original philosophy version during the program in hardcopy or electronic format to consolidate lessons learned. An organization could compile mentorship philosophies at the start, midpoint, and conclusion of the formalized relationship to conduct qualitative analysis about themes. The philosophical discernment process can guide program decisions at individual or collective levels.

Philosophical Reflection Areas

As a mentorship philosophy can synthesize principles for thoughts or actions, honest introspection can involve personal needs, interests, and preferences. The authenticity can stem from responses to shared questions, but probing and feedback from counterparts could be effective to navigate biases. First, personal needs can represent areas of criticality or higher importance for the developmental trajectory. A necessity could be safety from physical, mental, and emotional domains through respectful treatment. The compassion from a mentor or mentee to the counterpart could be essential for participants to share honest thoughts. As safety could involve perception, fostering an open communication channel can provide comfort for any individual to offer sentiments about the experience. An additional necessity could be resources for participation in programming activities. The relevant materials could include technological devices, conferencing platform licenses, professional development funds, note-taking supplies, or any items for enhanced accessibility. The needs could emerge from conversations as learner challenges could differ and remain concealed as invisible factors. Another necessity is the accommodation of programming based on identified learning barriers. For instance, instructional interventions could involve transcription software, speech-to-text communication devices, visual aids, language translation interfaces, and portfolio templates. A program design may consider cultural identities such as religious holidays or relational dynamics to model responsive action. The essential nature of needs grounds a philosophy with the foundational and must-have areas.

Second, interests can consolidate the stimulating or aspirational facets of the learning inventory for participants. An interest could be a social cause that imparts consequences for broader community members. The articulation of salient challenges can evoke a call to action for mentors or mentees to build capacity. An additional interest could be a professional or personal pathway for improved self-actualization. The identification of future career opportunities, educational achievements, and intended lifestyles can highlight the underlying motivations. Another interest could be activities that complement or expand the portfolio of existing abilities. For example, volunteerism, art showcases, sports competitions, traveling, and journaling could provide outlets for expression, collaboration, or mental health. As needs represent the must-have components, interests broaden the thinking to the should-have elements for the given individual.

Third, preferences can signify the prioritized areas when evaluating available options for decision-making. A preference may stem from initiative considerations of interaction frequency, relationship length, and program modality. The connection norms may depend on availability or intention, so discussion can enact clarity about selections. An additional preference could emerge from the matchup process as specific counterpart knowledge, skills, or experiences may complement the current candidate profile. The purposeful suggestion about identity elements could offer connection possibilities, but individuals may not recognize the best interests for the self. An alternate perspective from program facilitators could strategically balance preferences with needs to maximize learning. Another preference may be the adopted facilitative strategies or engagement techniques from the mentor or mentee counterpart respectively. The designated value for specific behaviors may originate from successful experiences or learning challenges, but a mentorship philosophy must be tailored. The preferences delve into participant heuristics as the could-have possibilities, while precise communication highlights personal tendencies. An honest and comprehensive mentorship philosophy considers needs, interests, and preferences (Figure 5.2).

| Needs | Interests | Preferences |

Figure 5.2 An overview of philosophical reflection areas. (Developed by Amelia Knop.)

Philosophical Manifestation into Mentorship Styles

Through the initial self-reflection and constructive discourse about unique participant philosophies, improved awareness can emerge about relevant mentorship styles. A philosophical perspective consolidates the underlying system of beliefs to influence decision-making and sense-making responsibilities. The philosophies of multiple participants can demonstrate convergence in some pillars and divergence in alternative areas. In contrast to visible mentorship styles, the philosophical elements may be invisible, internalized, or discrete. To articulate an abstract artifact in concrete terms, categorization through needs, interests, and preferences could be a recommended strategy. For instance, a mentee may need positive reinforcement to build confidence and multimodal interaction techniques to maximize introspection. The mentee may be interested in pursuing a position of increased responsibility in the organization and aspire to volunteer to support a specific identity group. The mentee may prefer to meet weekly for three months and complete collaborative inquiry projects. As the three clusters exhibit operational activities, the summative philosophical articulation could convey guiding themes as a strategic statement. The identified mentee appears to embrace compassion, accessibility, opportunity, servant leadership, and experience as resonating facets within the learning orientation. The unique composition may evolve from values, skills, and characteristics as a personal profile.

As a precise understanding of philosophical underpinnings could be necessary to deliberately shape the execution of mentorship techniques, a lack of awareness may prompt style activation at a subconscious level.

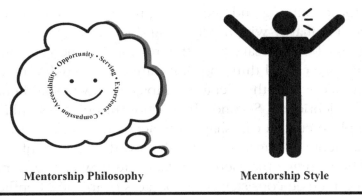

Mentorship Philosophy   Mentorship Style

Figure 5.3   An overview of mentorship philosophy and style. (Developed by Amelia Knop.)

The mentorship style can represent the specific dispositions from an individual within a learning relationship. Although a participant may initially attempt to leverage a given style, the implementation strategies could unintentionally mobilize alternative approaches. The adaptability could be valuable to navigate evolving organizational complexities and sensitivities, but misjudgment could simultaneously lead to unideal program outcomes. The manifestation of styles could encompass questioning techniques, thematic framing, linguistic conventions, and instructional tactics. An adopted mentor style considers the facilitation of knowledge, skills, and experiences for the mentee counterpart as the primary element, but still requires personal learning areas. A selected mentee style emphasizes the discernment and growth process through facilitative interactions, but still encourages sharing best practices with the mentor counterpart. As relationships are dynamic and stylistic combinations could be reframed after each interaction, ongoing reflection about program goals can center approach application (Figure 5.3).

Framing Appropriate Styles through Objectives

As limitless mentorship style permutations exist, participants must think carefully about the appropriate style based on both the matchup and program objectives. Although the co-construction process may illuminate differentiated priorities, the goals can be allocated into two overarching areas. First, the task pillar of building intellectual capacity can influence the method for identifying and exchanging relevant content. If a mentee exhibits lower familiarity with the learning domain, a style with increased involvement may be necessary from the mentor. If a mentee conveys an interest to improve critical thinking skills, a mentor may leverage a flipped learning approach where the mentee completes activities and engages in reflection at debriefing. Second, the relationship pillar of cultivating a healthy workplace culture can shape interactional and perspective-taking activities. If a mentee navigates relationships with higher confidence, the mentor could encourage the mentee to facilitate new connections across the institution. If a mentee consistently encounters or initiates conflict within an organizational unit, the mentor could tactfully pose reflection questions to ignite awareness about situational triggers. The link between mentorship style and program objectives is valuable to ensure intervention alignment.

Transformational Mentorship Styles

An investigation about transformational styles can encourage ideation for program participants about possible interventions. The transformational outlook can be viewed as a technique that seeks to generate stakeholder impact through the disruption of status quo practices. The strategies can spark improvement for community members from intellectual capacity and workplace culture domains, where the changes can be significant and long-lasting. To effectively create positive change, mentors and mentees must engage in collaborative dialogue to highlight critical opportunities for development. An appreciation for the interconnected nature of diverse organizational phenomena reinforces a need to pinpoint the underlying roots for maximum return on resource investment. The transformative orientation views the collaborative entity as a priority, whereas transactional activities may position the self before the counterpart. Although the transformational connotation may be heroic and glamorous, the willingness to embark on unprecedented change can be challenging. If the implications alter power dynamics or reposition comfortable individuals, the program participants may encounter resistance or pressure. As a result, authenticity and courage may be necessary within the mentor and mentee profiles (Figure 5.4).

First, the questioning innovator represents a style of lifelong learning and curiosity. The individual demonstrates an aptitude to pose thoughtful questions in response to organizational or broader community situations.

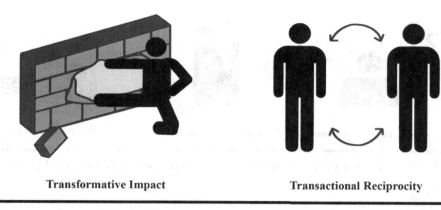

| Transformative Impact | Transactional Reciprocity |

Figure 5.4   An overview of transformational and transactional styles. (Developed by Amelia Knop.)

Despite the determination to challenge current or anticipated future practices, the participant must be tactful to cultivate community support. An inquiry could leverage open-ended techniques to spark higher-level thinking, while examination could occur through viewing, interaction, and output sources. The innovator identity is embedded as the style must leverage the compiled insights to implement compelling solutions with available resources. A mentor could adopt the style in facilitative conversations with the counterpart. The member could articulate reflection questions to ignite introspection and offer guidance about next steps. A mentee could embody the style in the expressed sentiments at program sessions. The individual may illuminate issues from empirical evidence and suggest actions to mitigate barriers.

Second, the quiet role model challenges the perception that change makers must be extraverted and dominating in organizational activities. The identified role model consistently conveys values-based behaviors with integrity, humility, and conscientiousness. Although the individual may not be in the spotlight, the generated impact can still be significant and even increased relative to more visible styles. The ongoing participant behaviors may converge with the personal identity as the member applies the resonating values across contexts. A mentor could adopt the style through daily interactions or decisions as the counterpart and community members can observe the best practices. A mentee could embody the style with an enthusiastic commitment to professional and personal growth. The determination to cultivate new skills can inspire the mentor counterpart, while initiating a contagious culture grounded in improvement.

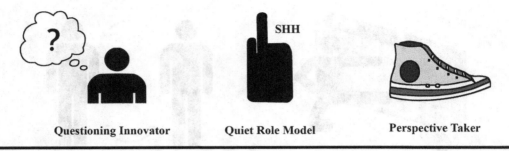

Figure 5.5 **An overview of transformational style categories. (Developed by Amelia Knop.)**

Third, the perspective taker considers the viewpoints of diverse stakeholders in an empathetic manner to enhance organizational accessibility. As a contemporary institution may seek to improve representation, belongingness, and fairness, attention to unique positionalities through active listening is vital. The ability to think critically from alternative standpoints can accumulate valuable insights about encountered barriers. An individual from a traditionally privileged background may require training or dialogue to enhance awareness. The care to initiate and maintain relationships with diverse individuals can reveal invisible considerations for authentic change. A mentor can adopt the style through engagement in the relationship as a collaborator and not only as a directive expert. A mentee can embody the style with a motivation to pinpoint biases and assumptions to extend understanding. The transformational styles can collectively showcase impact-driven activities and be blended for a personal mentorship identity (Figure 5.5).

Transactional Mentorship Styles

An exploration about transactional styles can create awareness for program participants regarding implementation alternatives. The transactional classification can be interpreted as a technique where participants help the counterpart but expect reciprocity in support. The styles could have positive or negative associations based on the participant's intentions. A transactional connection could prompt collaborative benefits as both members achieve goals that may not be possible in isolation. The success emerges due to the exchange of best practices, which reinforces the bidirectional framing of mentorship. As individuals recognize the advantages of continued partnership, repeated interaction can transpire over time. A transactional setting could become restrictive if individuals make decisions solely to match the perceived value provided from the counterpart. As opposed to exceeding the received best practices in a subsequent action, a participant could limit the response to align with the prior benefit level. The relationship could prioritize self-interest in decision-making and quickly dissipate due to frustration. As a result, transactional styles require facilitators to monitor progress and rectify issues promptly.

First, the goal setter focuses on achievement of specified benchmarks or aspirations through complementary supporting activities involving a counterpart. The individual seeks relevant resources from the mentorship relationship to pursue the objectives, while returning the exchange with similarly valued materials for the collaborator. Although a participant may spark a positive impact for the connected individual, an underlying interaction intention is to accomplish self-identified goals. The engagement in a mentorship matchup may depend on the perceived ability for the counterpart to enhance objective success. A mentor could adopt the style in learning from individuals with novel experiences and consequently offer best practices. A mentee could embody the style in registering for programs to compile specialized competences with awareness about unique abilities that could be provided as part of the learning transaction.

Second, the reward distributor offers or withholds recognition, resources, or opportunities to motivate best practice exchange from mentorship stakeholders. The participants may think strategically about tangible or intangible items that could be used for a bargain. An individual may have direct control over rewards that could be leveraged or need to engage in a network of transactions to mobilize aspects of interest for the counterpart. The information asymmetry could influence members to share specialized insights as a trade for alternative acumen. A mentor in a traditional relationship could adopt the style through providing awards, funds, equipment, or promotion recommendations. A mentee in a peer relationship could embody the style with new networking possibilities or favorable reviews for willingness to disseminate knowledge in a developmental area. The agreements could be implied or explicitly conveyed in transactions.

Third, the diligent organizer establishes a clear structure for the mentorship relationship to ensure mutual benefit for participants. An individual could determine a session schedule with time specifically and equitably allocated to achieving the goals of each member. The articulation

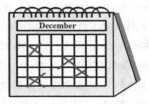

| Goal Setter | Reward Distributor | Diligent Organizer |

Figure 5.6   An overview of transactional style categories. (Developed by Amelia Knop.)

of boundaries for the connection is adopted to ensure participants recognize expectations in an evident manner. A balanced design reinforces that individuals have distinct interests and may only be motivated to engage in future interactions if progress ensues. An equitable structure does not necessarily represent equality, as allocations may depend on the perceived relative value of an exchange. A mentor can adopt the style through assuming responsibility for meeting agendas, while a mentee could articulate progress metrics for the relationship. As a result of developed philosophies, individuals may synthesize transactional and transformational areas in styles (Figure 5.6).

Collaborative Formulation and Revision of Living Artifacts

After an individual reflects about salient mentorship styles, the techniques can be integrated in the developed professional and personal statement with the identified philosophy. A collaborative process can be activated where participant counterparts ask questions and offer feedback, while the candidate annotates the multimodal artifact. The ongoing interactions can prompt revisions as a living document to consolidate the developmental journey. The analysis process can enact transformational and transactional styles as individuals spark metacognition about impact and reciprocity. As lifelong learners, the habit of revisiting identity artifacts can illuminate progress in prioritized and unforeseen domains. An intention of a mentorship program can be to reaffirm existing individual practices or posit refinement after re-examination.

Consolidation of Mentorship Styles and Philosophies

An understanding about relevant techniques for mentorship relationships requires an appreciation for underlying philosophical principles. The awareness about needs, interests, and preferences can guide the development of a multimodal mentorship philosophy, while outlining themes for initial program discussions. A cognizance for transformational and transactional styles can illustrate activities for generating change and exchanging insights equitably. The alignment of techniques with task and relationship goals can enhance progress. The resonating stylistic and philosophical aspects can influence the process of establishing connection norms.

Chapter 6

Building Relationships and Establishing Norms

As mentorship interventions involve organizational units with unique philosophies and aspirations, the exploration of possible strategies for cultivating relationships is necessary. The successful initiation of a connection can provide the foundation for a successful program, while co-construction of realistic norms can address any emergent tensions over time. This chapter outlines activities to strengthen mentorship collaborations and permit continued progress as the relationship factors change. A productive and supportive relationship blends the opportunity to extend intellectual capacity with a healthy culture of meaningful assistance. The perceptive aspect of relationships signifies that individuals may view productivity and support within the same connection to divergent degrees. As a result, norms for communication and activities can establish avenues for reconciliation. The compatibility of relationship experiences can shape the prospective achievements and interactions, so specific attention at the preliminary phase can orient a positive trajectory. As an action plan should consolidate the next steps, the collaboratively identified norms could clarify the acceptable techniques for ideation, revision, and execution in the organizational context. The dialogue about participant learning styles and intelligence can extract applicable pillars from the mentorship philosophy to personalize the developmental experience. Although building relationships and establishing norms may seem simplistic, the proficiency to adapt based on dyadic components is critical for a differentiated approach.

DOI: 10.4324/9781032715247-7

The guiding questions motivate program stakeholders from the mentorship community to think critically or creatively about best practices for constructing and maintaining relationships. First, individuals should consider: What norms and objectives are important for organizational mentorship initiatives, and why? At the start of a novel mentorship connection, norms do not yet exist as no commonly accepted practices are consolidated. The breadth for expressed standards is wide in scope as individuals could suggest diverse options. Any possibilities could stem from both past positive experiences and resonating improvement areas for encountered challenges. The alignment of norms and objectives is essential to ensure that relationship conditions can facilitate progress toward intended achievements. An ongoing discussion between mentorship program participants and administrators is valuable to accentuate priorities. As norms become solidified over time, individuals should engage in honest communication to express any issues or resistance. The ability to pivot earlier in norm development may be simpler than after practices are adopted. Second, practitioners should consider: How can knowledge about counterpart participant identities enhance relationship building, and why? As viewing, interactional, and output data sources provide insights about a mentorship community member, the aggregated knowledge can inform relationship development strategies. The awareness about visible and invisible identities can highlight approaches that would be conducive or ineffective in any given context. Although the specification of techniques may still be speculative, the inclusion of identity-based perspectives could possibly increase likelihood of appropriate selection. An appreciation for unique positionalities can offer context about the interpretive lenses of counterparts. As a result, cultivating relationships and norms can be an iterative, gradual, and collaborative process (Figure 6.1).

Productive   Supportive

Figure 6.1   An overview of productive and supportive areas. (Developed by Amelia Knop.)

Productive Relationship Strategies

Through ideation about approaches to develop effective relationships, mentorship participants can specify and personalize compelling strategies. The productivity element can represent the ability to achieve co-constructed objectives in a timely and positive manner. First, individuals can identify stages with progress metrics and contingency buffers. As ambitious goals in professional and personal domains may be multi-faceted, precise recognition of phases can ensure appropriate advancement. The activity stages should consider timeframes, sequences, responsibilities, and resources to comprehensively spark ideation. A timeframe can capture the deadline for completion of applicable milestones, while sequences can illustrate dependencies to determine prerequisite tasks. The responsibilities are necessary to recognize which relationship participants should assume initiative. A brainstorm about available resources, constraints, and necessary procurement can influence awareness about the likely project trajectory. The stages should be complemented with quantitative and qualitative metrics to confirm progress beyond a surface-level estimation. A strategic allocation of contingency time or resources can ensure that participants are not under pressure if unanticipated challenges transpire. Second, members should specify goals with priority weightings and consider blended contexts. The articulation of objectives and subsequent display using visible artifacts can generate shared understanding in the mentorship community. The identification of relative importance is valuable so that participants know expectations about achievement to appropriately allocate attention. As intellectual capacity and healthy culture are both integral, an objective could be prioritized for each categorization.

Third, mentorship collaborators should use time efficiently within interaction meetings and articulate clear parameters for activities. As individuals may possess busy schedules and opportunities for live sessions could be limited, planning is critical to maximize learning. A mentorship agreement could specify relationship responsibilities such as scheduling meetings, distributing agendas, organizing experiences, and summarizing action items. The integration of a session breakdown with appropriate time for ideation, reflection, and execution could ensure that objectives are not neglected. A free time segment could be retained for individuals to delve deeper into areas of interest. If session elements are ambiguous, too much time may be allocated to a particular area and result in less discussion about

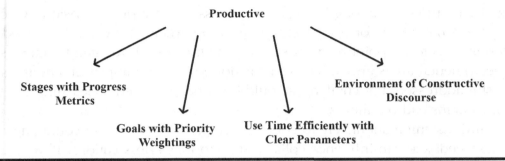

Figure 6.2 **An overview of productive relationship strategies. (Developed by Amelia Knop.)**

a similarly important component. Fourth, relationship members should cultivate an environment of constructive discourse. If individuals collectively decide to articulate honest perceptions in a respectful manner, then participants can analyze and evaluate resonating challenges. The willingness to show appropriate vulnerability and discuss issues can spark thinking about possible solutions. If the individuals do not explicitly express that healthy conflict is permissible, misalignment in expectations may emerge. A conflict may occur if mutual understanding is not generated, which could influence member engagement (Figure 6.2).

Supportive Relationship Strategies

The consideration about techniques to cultivate supportive relationships represents the aptitude to assist counterparts with professional or personal challenges in an appropriate manner. First, providing encouragement and celebrating successes are meaningful strategies to generate positivity within a mentorship program. The genuine communication of motivational remarks can impart confidence and inspire individuals to achieve at a higher standard. As participants may be accustomed to constructive feedback, allocating time to provide positive comments can spark a new sense of determination in challenging moments. An authentic sentiment can involve specificity within the message content and enthusiasm from a delivery standpoint. The attention to detail through recalling milestones, giving mementos, expressing gratitude, and highlighting achievements can facilitate connectivity. Second, focusing on strengths in feedback sessions can tactfully address improvements with aspirational framing. A tendency may be to articulate a long listing of weaknesses that require revision, which may be demotivating or overwhelming for the participant. A recommended alternative is to pinpoint relevant strengths that can be leveraged to address developmental areas and co-construct action plans. The improvement areas are still addressed, but challenges could be conceptualized as learning moments instead of failures.

Third, listening attentively to counterpart experiences and encouraging honest feedback can influence collaborators to focus on solutions. If an individual is disengaged or inadvertently dominates in conversations, the opportunity to pinpoint best practices and compile personalized knowledge could be missed. The commitment to processing insights can require members to minimize distractions, ask probing questions, and synthesize themes. Through concentration and confidentiality in dialogue, participants may feel comfortable to express honest thoughts about deeper issues. An individual should simultaneously invite the counterpart to express feedback about the relationship experience to consistently improve interventions. Fourth, allocating time regularly to ensure well-being adopts a person-centered learning approach. A periodic check-in can provide opportunities for participants to seek strategies for improved physical, mental, and emotional health. Although an inclination may be to proceed promptly with the task elements in a mentorship session, initial dialogue should prioritize the wellness of the individuals. As participants may have divergent comfort levels, the platform for sharing should be activated but members should not be pressured to offer updates. If a relationship continues to strengthen over time, the participants could be more likely to discuss concerns. The awareness of productive and supportive relationship strategies can invite success when tailored to individual identities (Figure 6.3).

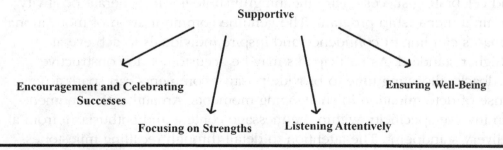

Figure 6.3 An overview of supportive relationship strategies. (Developed by Amelia Knop.)

Motivation for Relationship Continuation

After a mentorship relationship is initiated, the perceived learning value for participants may shape whether the connection proceeds until or extends beyond the formally suggested end date. A possible factor is motivation of the collaborators, which considers the sources to ignite participation or effort toward a specified behavior. First, intrinsic motivation can represent the sources within or internal to an identified individual. A mentorship philosophy may orient an individual about resonating values and evoke self-awareness to engage in the sense-making of relationship value. The aptitude for lifelong learning can influence participation as the mentor or mentee candidate compiles new knowledge, skills, and experiences. The evident lessons can be applied to professional and personal activities in a cross-disciplinary manner. A responsibility to continue improving salient abilities may inspire an individual to accept feedback and pursue higher standards of achievement. The interpretation of positionality as a vocation can blend activities with identity to improve effectiveness. A sense of self-actualization may transpire as individuals share best practices with counterparts to spark broader community impact. The new relationship can enhance belongingness and expand a personal network. As the intrinsic category is aspirational, the motivators can align with improving intellectual capacity and healthy culture.

Second, extrinsic motivation can signify the sources beyond or external to a specific individual. Although the motivation techniques may consequently prompt growth in task and relationship areas, individuals who focus only on extrinsic sources may not be authentically engaged in a learning connection. A monetary stipend for participation could provide resources for individuals to assemble new materials, pursue professional development, or reduce the burden of forgoing alternate commitments. The recognition for completing the program or improving in performance metrics could be offered through certificates, advancements, or praise. Although the acknowledgment can be valuable, a humility in professional and personal endeavors may be necessary for growth at a deeper level. Participation in a relationship to strategically expand the professional network and improve social capital could be meaningful to mobilize resources or uncover opportunities. Although intrinsic and extrinsic motivators may both apply within mentorship programs, facilitators must consider the implementation

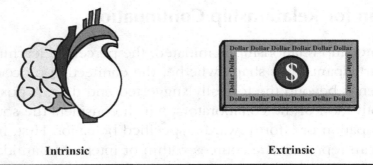

Intrinsic   Extrinsic

Figure 6.4   An overview of intrinsic and extrinsic motivators. (Developed by Amelia Knop.)

implications. If a source only sparks temporary change, then administrators should redesign mentorship conditions (Figure 6.4).

Interest for Relationship Continuation

As mentorship programs may have mandatory or voluntary structures in diverse organizational environments, individuals may demonstrate varied levels of initial interest. A mandatory context should allocate additional time to learning about the needs and preferences of participants to cultivate meaningful connections from the outset. The integration of open-ended questions, team-building activities, and ideation sessions in a preliminary phase can illustrate relevant considerations about personal identity. A strategic matchup process is necessary to ensure appropriate alignment in aspirations, which can promote natural conversation. A voluntary landscape may appear to assemble individuals with initiative as involvement is not required, but introspection about underlying visible and invisible motivators is helpful. The statement of interest can support discernment, while interviews and recommendations can provide additional context for the learner profile. As relationships progress in mandatory or voluntary programs, check-in sessions with guiding questions can identify positive and constructive areas. To compile relevant data for program interventions, participants could provide anonymized responses to the administrators for thematic analysis. The interest in learning opportunities may increase over time and in diverse trajectories, so offering space for relationship-building can be important. A culture of honest communication can illuminate experiences within relationships or programs.

Co-Construction Process for Norms and Expectations

The collaborative identification of relationship guidelines or boundaries can offer shared understanding for participants about acceptable behaviors. A productive and supportive relationship requires that members proceed consistently in a manner that benefits both organizational units. A norm can represent a typical or anticipated categorization of actions. For instance, a mentor and mentee may decide to distribute an agenda for the next meeting at least one week in advance using a selected communication platform. After the behavior is repeated on multiple occasions, the participants may recognize the action as an unwritten or implied element. Although repetition of a given activity can be positive if participants are both in agreement, undesirable behaviors may become internalized if not addressed in a timely manner. As a result, the opening stages of a relationship require open dialogue to express thoughts and feelings about conducted actions. A mentorship expectation could be viewed similarly as a specific situation or behavior that is predictable moving forward. The relationship expectations should be managed appropriately to ensure satisfaction for both collaborators. For example, a mentee may send messages to a mentor and expect responses within 24 hours. However, the mentor could be a senior-level manager who may be delayed and respond within the week unless the request is urgent. A misalignment in the expectations may prompt frustration but could be addressed through dialogue in the early phase.

As participant intentions may be harmless and individuals may not recognize that adopted behaviors hinder the relationship, common themes are captured to guide norm identification. First, members should articulate one to three overarching goals for the program. The explanation of significance to another individual can cultivate an understanding about a mentorship philosophy. Second, participants should clearly specify the program structural areas such as interaction frequency, relationship length, and exchange modality. Any program requirements could be compared to collaborator preferences to establish a foundation. Third, individuals should convey responsibilities for session planning, facilitation, and debriefing. The allocation of formal roles or decision to rotate tasks could be mutually determined to maximize value from participation. Fourth, members should explore the scope of topics and experiential learning activities. If the mentor or mentee expresses a preference to only focus on professional areas, the stakeholders can ensure appropriate boundaries are followed. Fifth, participants should explain communication and learning strategies based on unique needs, interests, or preferences. The dialogue can evoke self-awareness about approaches to maximize growth with consideration for past experiences. Sixth, individuals should describe possible resource allocations so that decisions are strategically executed. The availability of financial, human, intellectual, physical, and technological resources could shape relationship activities. Seventh, the mentor and mentee should outline procedures to resolve any possible conflicts. Although disagreements may not occur, proactive ideation can generate a toolkit of approaches for positive resolution. Eighth, the collaborators should suggest timeframes to review and adjust norms based on progress within the onboarding phase. As each relationship has a special identity, topics could be added or removed based on member insights (Figure 6.5).

The description of a possible process for co-constructing preliminary norms can be applied within the onboarding session. If a matchup is announced before an orientation meeting, the mentor and mentee can individually brainstorm preferences for norms. The exercise is not intended to provide a baseline for negotiation and should instead be viewed as an opportunity for introspection about respective viewpoints. To build a genuine relationship, individuals should allocate the first moments to learning about the counterpart if prior familiarity does not exist.

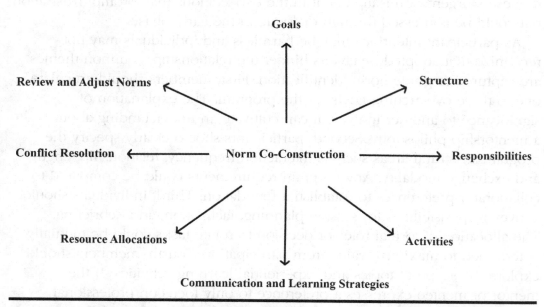

Figure 6.5   An overview of norm co-construction themes. (Developed by Amelia Knop.)

A subsequent stage is to engage in ideation about all possibilities for the template topics. A program facilitator may decide to adapt the themes to the organizational context and distribute models to guide discussion. An exhaustive list of alternatives for the expected behaviors could be articulated to minimize hesitation for participants about sharing honest perspectives. The members could proceed through the topics and determine a shortlist of resonating options. A selected norm for each category could be stored in a multimodal format for future reference. The relationship objectives could be outlined within the artifact to orient the connection trajectory. If individuals are unsure about norms, multiple options could be listed temporarily and attempted in the upcoming sessions. After a specific timeframe has passed, the participants could revisit the norms and participate in constructive discourse about revisions. Although co-construction of norms may be perceived as time-consuming, benefits can appear later in the relationship.

Co-Construction Process for Compelling Action Plans

After norms and expectations are thoughtfully considered, relationship participants have a common understanding necessary to proceed with achievement of articulated objectives. An action plan can represent a clear specification of stages and milestones to progress successfully within the relationship parameters. A plan can be identified promptly through ideation, but the approach has the potential to be more compelling if relevant criteria are satisfied. First, the identified activity should be productive and directly link to overarching goals. If the success factors, timeframes, and resources are appropriately conveyed, individuals will recognize how to advance. Second, supportive interventions such as tailored assistance, resources, and mitigation strategies can retain progress if adversities emerge. An evaluation of worst-case scenarios with best-case outcomes can highlight the continuum of possibilities to spark ongoing metacognition. Third, the motivational sources should be aligned to maximize accountability. An appropriate challenge level is critical to avoid boredom and mitigate unhealthy anxiety. Fourth, authentic interest can stem from co-construction where both members are meaningfully involved. If plans are productive, supportive, motivational, and interesting, any relationship can prosper.

An investigation of possible action plan types can provide mentors and mentees with options to evaluate in a brainstorming session. First, an external gap-oriented plan focuses on imparting change for a current

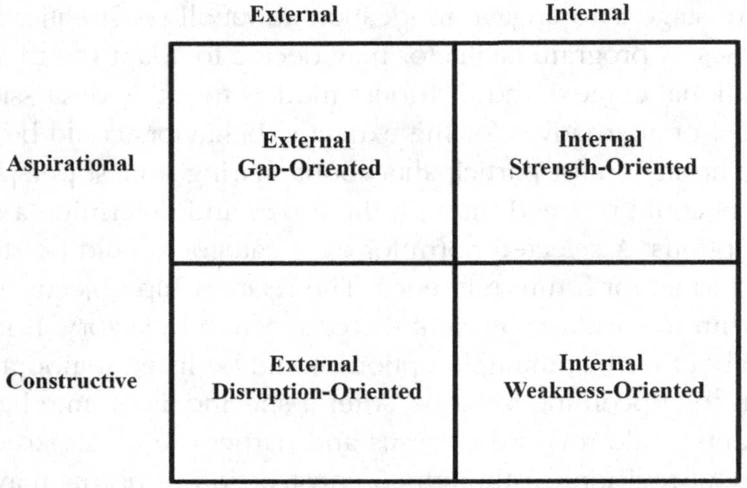

	External	Internal
Aspirational	External Gap-Oriented	Internal Strength-Oriented
Constructive	External Disruption-Oriented	Internal Weakness-Oriented

Figure 6.6 An overview of action plan types. (Developed by Amelia Knop.)

missing area in the organizational landscape. For instance, an individual may aspire to initiate a new professional learning community for employees who intend to pursue positions of additional responsibility. Second, an external disruption-oriented plan emphasizes activities that challenge the status quo for improvement in the organizational ecosystem. For example, a member may advocate for enhanced accessibility to professional development opportunities for traditionally disadvantaged identities. Third, an internal strength-oriented plan prioritizes opportunities to leverage and refine existing positive traits for the self. For instance, an individual may hope to extend proficient communication skills to an even higher level through guidance from an experienced counterpart. Fourth, an internal weakness-oriented plan seeks to address shortfalls or challenges within the present personal portfolio. For example, a member may struggle with self-confidence and benefit from strategies to contribute ideas more effectively within team projects. The consideration of action plans for external and internal domains with aspirational or constructive framing can generate concrete next steps in learning (Figure 6.6).

Recognition of Learning Styles and Intelligences

The appreciation of learning styles can guide mentors and mentees in activities that facilitate professional or personal growth. A learning style can represent a technique that optimizes sense-making and thinking for relationship participants. As individuals will exhibit unique identities, the strengths and weaknesses could diverge across members. The recognition of styles can stem from viewing or conversing, where the counterpart may share experiences. First, a sight style emphasizes observation of visual artifacts and demonstrations to accumulate new knowledge. A mentor could provide resource guides, simulate examples in a live format, or adopt non-verbal cues to generate novel insights. Second, a hearing style focuses on listening attentively to sounds from individuals or broader surroundings. A mentee could concentrate on instructions that are shared from a counterpart or consider noises in each setting to interpret phenomena. Third, an experiential style prioritizes the opportunity to attempt activities and proceed with repetition as needed to improve competency. A mentor could invite a mentee sports athlete to try a new skill and facilitate debriefing after appropriate practice intervals. A member may change styles within and across contexts, but awareness about needs can guide instructional decisions. The ability to align styles can improve through dialogue in the learning relationship.

An attention to learning intelligences can expand possibilities for complementary development in a bidirectional exchange. Intelligence can be framed as a distinguishing competency in a knowledge or skill area. The differentiation may occur comparatively to other intelligences within a person or relative to the proficiency levels of alternative community members. First, an intelligence may be specialized within a particular learning environment. An individual can display significant understanding of an academic discipline such as organizational behavior, historical literature, international law, environmental economics, anatomy, or machine learning. The higher threshold of competency could occur due to blended factors such as educational training, professional experience, or personal interest activities. Second, an intelligence may be generalized across learning contexts and facilitate adaptability. A member could possibly possess effective numeracy, literacy, decision-making, leadership, communication, conflict resolution, or collaboration abilities. The versatile capability could guide a mentor from one department to impart relevant best practices for a mentee from a distinct organizational unit with divergent specialty knowledge. A culture of open dialogue and expression can incentivize participants to share hidden abilities, while deepening the learning exchange in areas of mutual development.

Consolidation of Building Relationships and Establishing Norms

A willingness to think critically and creatively about appropriate strategies for building relationships can maximize success for mentorship program participants. Although norms can evolve naturally, the implementation of purposeful and ongoing conversations at an early stage can foster shared understanding. A productive and supportive relationship grounded in motivation and interest has the possibility to achieve unparalleled outcomes. The involvement of mentors and mentees in identifying expectations, action plans, and learning factors can enhance the experience. A strong interpersonal foundation may result in a long-lasting connection.

Chapter 7

Before, During, and After Mentorship

A mentorship journey can include numerous stages and milestones that may emerge uniquely based on the relationship objectives, norms, or identities. Although each connection will possess divergent characteristics, common phases can be anticipated to guide sense-making about overarching progress. This chapter pinpoints typical mentorship activities that transpire between the program outset and relationship ending. A recognition about initial, ongoing, and concluding stages can influence decision-making about upcoming learning opportunities. The mentorship connection may appear as a linear progression, but organizational units can pivot through sub-phases, which represent an unpredictable pathway. A formal learning relationship could transform naturally into an informal platform for knowledge exchange for an undetermined time. As the connection norms are co-constructed and internalized, diverse techniques will resonate with the program participants. An understanding of appropriate segments to advise, encourage, ask, and challenge in a learning experience can depend on movement between relationship stages. The non-linear adventure may be simpler to interpret in the aftermath of a mentorship program, but metric evaluation and constructive dialogue during the activities can evoke increased awareness. A process for best practice exchange can involve pre-brief, live mentorship, and debrief conferencing sessions, which can formulate new insights for improved future action. As a result, the identification of learning stages can shape mentorship interventions.

DOI: 10.4324/9781032715247-8

The guiding questions invite mentorship participants to suggest relevant activities and achievements within developmental phases based on organizational program intentions. First, individuals should consider: What milestones display participant progress in a mentorship relationship, and why? An ideation session about relationship and program success could involve diverse stakeholders such as mentors, mentees, and initiative administrators. The appreciation for institutional conditions can illuminate factors that could enhance or constrain progress. Although a tendency may be to impose objectives for participants, a learner-centered model may encourage the directly impacted stakeholders to share initial expectations. The conversation and questioning activities could delve deeper into underlying rationale to align divergent perceptions of the program trajectory. The collaborative specification of milestones can be derived based on objectives and should consider the accumulated data to inform decision-making. As individuals will prioritize varied philosophies, styles, and values, the resonating themes can position a learning relationship within the broader program. Second, practitioners should consider: What activities are needed for the specific learner at each stage, and why? The articulation of general tasks or behaviors in the mentorship pathway can illustrate relative positioning for introspection about progress. A shared interpretation about sequencing can convey a compelling orientation for professional and personal growth. To maximize development for individuals from diverse identities, the general activities should be tailored to the specific learning landscape. A willingness to attempt new approaches can accumulate feedback about retention, revision, or removal of strategies. As the overarching program structure offers a starting point for planning and execution, the principles could be applied to launch initiatives in diverse organizations.

Initial, Ongoing, and Concluding Stage Activities

An overview of the mentorship relationship phases is necessary for participants and administrators to recognize progress. First, the initial stage can represent the opening activities of the intervention. The preceding planning requirements to offer a mentorship initiative could include candidate selection, resource allocation, matchup specification, and reporting tool development. An introduction can spark the connection-building process, where individuals have opportunities to share identities, objectives, aspirations, philosophies, and preferred norms. The program considerations of frequency, length, and modality are tentatively captured. Second, the ongoing stage can prioritize the experiential learning moments. The facilitation of discussion sessions, professional workshops, organizational exploration, and feedback exchange can expose participants to novel best practices. A check-in activity can be integrated at regular intervals to identify achievement based on co-constructed milestones, while appropriate adjustments may be applied after experience. Third, the concluding stage can consolidate learning and represent a termination of the formalized mentorship activities. The participants may synthesize and disseminate lessons learned through relevant institutional channels. If the relationship ends, the participants could express gratitude and convey farewell messages. As the collaborators may decide to continue the journey informally, a pivot to the prior learning phase could occur. An investigation of each phase with specificity can promote execution of program elements.

The initial stage consolidates the activities before and including the original mentorship meeting. The responsibilities may involve developing a program plan, facilitating a discernment process for candidates, and cultivating conditions for a strong connection foundation. If a prior program has not been implemented within the institution, the mentorship advocate would likely submit a proposal to the management team. An explanation of initiative goals may stem from the organizational values and vision statement, while rationale could encompass compiled data about growth opportunities. After approval is received, the program facilitator should identify the number of mentors and mentees. A decision about whether participation is mandatory and if applications will be collected can influence relevant messaging to intended stakeholders. The selection criteria can guide determination of the mentorship pool, while matchups can be finalized manually or using automated software. An executive-level session about available financial, human, intellectual, physical, and technological resources can offer a preliminary portfolio for implementation. Any applicable data collection mechanisms could be activated to compile initial perceptions for longitudinal comparison. The opening message could be sent to the mentors, mentees, and supporting collaborators to outline formal program expectations. An orientation meeting could be scheduled as a group or dyad with guiding prompts. The individuals should have the possibility to share professional and personal identities where comfortable to ignite interpersonal learning. A preliminary ideation session about individualized goals and anticipated success factors can clarify the relationship scope.

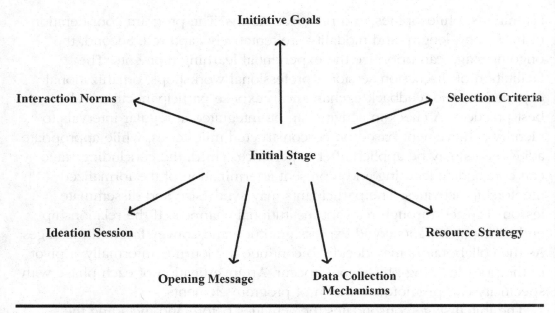

Figure 7.1   An overview of initial stage considerations. (Developed by Amelia Knop.)

The co-construction of interaction norms can explicitly illustrate appropriate behaviors to maximize productivity and support. The initiation may be viewed as a new beginning where participants navigate a novel environment (Figure 7.1).

The ongoing stage assembles the learning interventions that occur deliberately or spontaneously for relationship stakeholders. The mentors and mentees are actively involved in exercises, but program facilitators or administrators may have implementation responsibilities. An experiential opportunity could be an excursion to an alternative location or shadowing day within a new department to gain exposure to diverse perspectives. The compiled aspirations in the initiation stage can guide the identification, evaluation, and recommendation of action steps. A discussion session could occur through in-person or virtual modalities to share experiences, accomplishments, lessons learned, and inquiry questions. The dialogue can explore underlying issues, possible alternatives, and implementation stages to address task and relationship areas. A professional workshop could involve a guest speaker, external accreditation agency, or internal organizational seminar on specialized interests. The platform to process unique knowledge, skills, and experiences can be complemented with mentorship debriefing. An organizational showcase could permit individuals to present resonating insights, while mentees could pursue opportunities to shadow mentors in novel learning areas. The feedback exchange could transpire through multimodal pathways, where the mentor asks probing questions and mentee conveys insights that shape professional or personal development. A living portfolio of best practices or catalog of learning activities can provide a journal for self-reflection about progress. The nature of activities may differ based on relationship or program factors, but the broadly illustrated techniques could guide instructional decision-making. Although the frequency and duration of interactions will diverge across connections, check-in sessions are consistently important to verify trajectories. An opportunity to revisit norms and objectives from the initial stage can recalibrate the relationship (Figure 7.2).

The concluding stage synthesizes growth from intellectual capacity and workplace culture domains. The timeframe can represent the final remaining activities within a relationship and scheduled termination of the connection before informal mentorship emerges. Although the concluding phase follows the ongoing segment, the length of core learning activities can depend on program requirements or mutual participant interest. A closure opportunity is necessary for individuals to reflect holistically on the learning journey. If a culmination session is neglected, members may miss the possibility to articulate resonating aspects to influence future learning relationships

Figure 7.2 An overview of ongoing stage considerations. (Developed by Amelia Knop.)

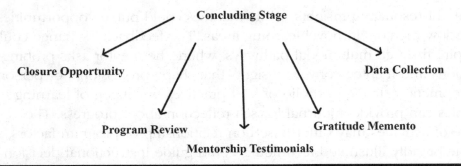

Figure 7.3   An overview of concluding stage considerations. (Developed by Amelia Knop.)

for either participant. A review of program successes and challenges can provide valuable information for program facilitators to consider in developmental planning. A lesson learned forum can invite individuals to offer best practices to a broader audience which may assist with cultivating a collaborative culture. The mentorship testimonials could be distributed with permission through organizational communication channels, while graduates may return to support subsequent program cycles. A gratitude memento such as a card or relationship artifact could be provided to reinforce appreciation for the counterpart. The initiative coordination team should distribute concluding data collection mechanisms to capture developmental changes from the program. After reporting is finished, a mentorship cycle could restart with new connections (Figure 7.3).

Transition from Formal to Informal Mentorship Relationships

Although individuals may engage in a formal mentorship program with conveyed requirements, participants may display interest to pursue an informal learning connection after the original conclusion date. The motivations to extend the relationship may include perceived value in best practice exchange, newly established friendship, collaboration possibilities, and positive developmental progress. To proceed with the matchup for the foreseeable future, members would need to exhibit mutual agreement of the next steps. A planning meeting could be organized in the formal concluding stages, where the individuals share thoughts about future norms, aspirations, and structures. An honest conversation is important to ensure alignment in interest as lack of balance in intentions could result in unproductive or unsupportive relations. The interpreted power dynamics in a traditional connection with a senior mentor and junior mentee could generate implied pressure. As a result, a learner-centered focus could permit mentees to suggest continuation if the interest exists. The new relationship stages may involve adjusted session frequencies, durations, and modalities based on evolving needs. A program administrator could consider asking participants about their willingness to continue a connection in advance of a conclusion meeting and promote dialogue for matchups with mutual interest.

Mentorship Techniques Portfolio

A grasp of strategies to maximize learning at relevant stages for both participants in the mentorship dyad can cultivate non-linear developmental opportunities. The expressed techniques can be applied collaboratively within a mentorship portfolio after consideration about member identities and needs. First, the advisory approach suggests best practices for counterpart sense-making without requirement for fulfillment. An individual can articulate possibilities based on applicable knowledge, skills, and experiences to spark ideation. The intention is to expand awareness about next steps to achieve co-constructed objectives or resolve any encountered challenges. The advisor's positionality can provide diverse insights for introspection and mobilize professional discretion to orient the collaborator. An advantage is the potential to disseminate novel perspectives to individuals who need timely assistance. However, a disadvantage is that counterparts may not engage deeply in critical thinking if solutions are quickly presented. The individuals must remember to pinpoint biases, assumptions, and boundary conditions that can impact the effectiveness of recommendations. Despite the ability to disseminate advice at any stage, receptivity could increase later in the relationship once referent power is fostered.

Second, the encouragement approach exhibits positive reinforcement, optimism, and support for counterpart learners. The aspirational sentiments could be shared for moments of success or challenge as the feedback can provide additional motivation. An attention to needs could possibly enhance performance or well-being at an individual level, while nurturing a collaborative culture grounded in lifelong growth. The blend of conveyed language and non-verbal dispositions could shape the interpretation of messaging authenticity. Consistency in interactions could establish psychological safety for honest expression in ongoing dialogue. However, encouragement does not represent offering positive comments only. The individual would still provide constructive feedback but could consider leveraging strengths to impart solutions. An advantage is the capability to reignite interest from a member at a critical inflection point, while a disadvantage is the possibility for a counterpart to self-assess progress unrealistically due to positive framing. The cultivation of trust requires time as individuals process relationship norms, so encouragement could start toward the end of initiation or at early learning core phases.

Third, the asking approach prepares and articulates thoughtful reflection questions to spark participant metacognition. The use of diverse formulations to establish facts, investigate resonating examples, and consolidate implications for individualized objectives can enrichen the sense-making conversation. A variation in closed and open-ended guiding prompts can ensure shared understanding about perceptions, while permitting opportunities to communicate honest viewpoints. Although a participant may tentatively determine questions to pose in a conferencing session, the expressed responses can prompt revisions at the moment. An adaptable or dynamic methodology can provide flexibility for facilitators to navigate the discussion trajectory in a natural manner. To effectively capture resonating insights, the individual must listen attentively to the articulated ideas from the counterpart and ask for clarification as required. An advantage is that asking questions in a tactful manner can uncover tacit perspectives or invisible elements within a learning experience. A disadvantage is information overload could overwhelm the questioner in the interpretive process since the weighting of importance could be challenging. As posing inquiries can extract personal insights, the technique could be used at any program stage.

Fourth, the challenger approach denotes the courage to oppose status quo situations in a quest for continued improvement. An individual should not assume an adversarial stance but could instead engage in collaborative inquiry to prioritize community gaps. The aptitudes to detect and spark change are not identical as distinct actions are necessary for each category. The identification step requires that participants think critically and creatively about current organizational phenomena. In contrast, the

| Advisory | Encouragement | Asking | Challenger |

Figure 7.4   A depiction of mentorship portfolio techniques. (Developed by Amelia Knop.)

subsequent activity to generate impact must leverage political or social capital in a strategic manner to navigate inherent constraints. The individual should adopt an aspirational framing to alter existing structures or barriers. An advantage is the commitment to disrupting internalized practices can offer improved solutions. The disadvantages include possible focus on self-interest and exclusion from future advancement due to conflict. As challenging views need relationship rapport, the behavior could increase in the later stages (Figure 7.4).

Learning Intervention Conferencing Milestones

A depiction of the relationship conferencing milestones can offer strategies to facilitate dialogue from the program initiation until conclusion. A conferencing session can represent the opportunity for participants to exchange best practices in verbal format. The process consistently includes pre-brief, live mentorship, and debrief elements. As mentorship relationships involve iterative learning moments, the three pillars could be repeated numerous times throughout a connection with multiple interventions. To promote reflection in advance and ensure comfort during a meeting, individuals could leverage written resources to complement the discussion. The purpose is to spark honest communication about perceptions and experiences to date within the relationship or broader learning community. The conferencing process can occur at any developmental level, so an overview of milestones can influence implementation tactics. As individuals foster a new connection or reignite a prior collaboration in the initiation phase, conferencing can clarify aspirations and learning strategies. The ongoing phase serves as the core for an experiential growth trajectory, where conferencing can generate novel insights. The concluding phase could mobilize conferencing techniques to synthesize best practices for future application. As a result, a conferencing approach can be valuable to evoke constructive discourse among participants and encourage perspective taking for learners at any growth zone.

First, the pre-brief milestone captures the necessary activities to be conducted before the learning intervention transpires. If a conferencing process has not yet occurred in a relationship, the participants can engage in ideation about specific learning outcomes. The opening dialogue may represent a diagnostic function as individuals express readiness, prior experience, and aspirations. For connections where the debrief milestone has already been completed once, the summative feedback report about next steps can guide learning priorities for the new iteration. The conversation could be diagnostic if a novel learning focus is adopted or formative if the session represents a continuation of previously explored topics. A pre-brief milestone offers an opportunity for participants to narrow the learning focus. For instance, a learning intervention with a specialized topic presentation may prioritize feedback about delivery style. Although the content possesses importance, emphasis on a given learning area can enhance quality progress in application and reflection. A series of open-ended questions could assemble learning goals, achievement indicators, and relevant resources in a constructivist manner. The conferencing could provide a comfortable forum for learners to seek clarification about unfamiliar areas. Any expressed perspectives could be recorded in a multimodal manner through the learning portfolio for future reference. The pre-brief strategy can reinforce the productive and supporting frame for the mentorship relationship, while imparting baseline understanding to proceed appropriately.

Second, the live mentorship milestone represents viewing, interaction, or output activities to exchange relevant insights. The mobilization of techniques such as advise, encourage, ask, and challenge could be interconnected within the developmental process. As individuals have diverse identities, relative prioritization of approaches could be differentiated for members. After the collaborative selection of a learning opportunity, the mentor could witness mentee behaviors from intellectual capacity and workplace culture standpoints. Depending on the identified mentorship strategies from the opening dialogue, the mentor could converse with the mentee at appropriate intervals to extract thoughts. Any outputs from the process could be reviewed and retained, while activation of multiple data collection techniques can enrichen debriefing. As the mentorship relationship focuses on facilitating learning and not formally assessing competency, mentees should be encouraged to proceed with normal conduct. The vulnerability of mentees could be necessary for authentic behavior to be displayed, so relationship intentions should be clearly established to ensure engagement. A learning opportunity could be completed in a formal or informal domain, such as the facilitation of a workshop or mentor observation of mentee activities in a typical day. The openness to experiences can be valuable as meaningful learning moments could emerge spontaneously without planning to complement intended segments. The focus for live mentorship is immersion of participants in a learning journey. An awareness about mentee needs can guide mentors to determine whether guidance, reinforcement, question, or change-based actions are most relevant for learning. As comprehensive insights are constructed through the identified experiences, reflection is a necessary sequential step to engage in sense-making.

Third, the debrief milestone occurs following a learning activity and pinpoints applicable lessons learned. A session could be organized for the mentor and mentee to focus specifically on how the learning experience supported growth from the pre-brief. The consolidation should be completed honestly with precise specifications of positive and constructive elements. A mentor should probe deeper to understand the underlying rationale and determine best practices for future application within or across contexts. The collaborative introduction of evidence from the process can supplement initial thinking about outcomes. A summative articulation about progress from the starting phase could build capacity, while illustrating remaining pathways for growth. As lifelong learners, the mentors should similarly pinpoint new insights from viewing or interacting in the intervention. The synthesis activities could serve as a summative task in the relationship or become formative if another learning intervention is identified to further expand skills. As a tendency may be to deviate between topics, specific attention to the activity should be maintained for evident closure. Although progress may not align with anticipated growth, significant development can still transpire. Through participation in the conferencing stages, the learning

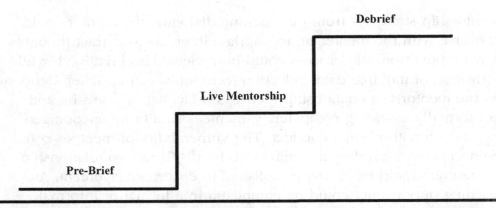

Figure 7.5   An overview of conferencing milestones. (Developed by Amelia Knop.)

process can be individualized to cultivate awareness about next steps for improvement (Figure 7.5).

Goal Achievement and Check-In Reflections

An appreciation for participant accomplishment and staged opportunities for reflection could support retention of best practices. A mentor or mentee can gain valuable knowledge in the moment, but authentic processing is important to promote long-term application. The explicit identification of successful goal completion can serve as positive reinforcement. A concluding activity could ask the relationship participants to highlight achievements, while the program administrators could embed resonating areas in a recognition artifact. To maximize possibilities for progress at the appropriate developmental zone, goals could possess meet and exceed levels. A self-assessment continuum may consolidate learning more clearly than a binary completion metric. As individuals may recognize new learning considerations as time proceeds, a check-in session could occur a few days after the debriefing milestone. The time and space to participate in metacognition about the reflection session can evoke deeper sentiments. Although an inclination may be to direct the conversation, mentors must exhibit restraint to evoke a mentee-centered model. The mentee should have the autonomy to express accumulated best practices and any remaining questions, which could be resolved in the meeting or through subsequent research (Figure 7.6).

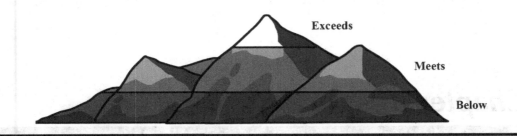

Figure 7.6 A depiction of achievement levels. (Developed by Amelia Knop.)

Consolidation of Before, During, and After Mentorship

The investigation of initial, ongoing, and concluding stages in a mentorship relationship can spark ideation about the diverse encountered activities. As learning facilitation requires planning, individuals are encouraged to consider whether interventions align with the identified connection phase. Each relationship may pursue a unique trajectory, so participants should explicitly discuss possible interests to continue the developmental opportunities. The application of diverse techniques can tailor learning, while conferencing milestones can delve into salient goals. A review of overall program stages can guide specific feedback exchange activities.

Chapter 8

Verbal and Written Feedback

As mentorship activities capture the bidirectional exchange of best practices between participants, an examination of considerations for disseminating feedback is important. The opportunity to provide and receive feedback can transfer insights across organizational units. This chapter consolidates verbal and written techniques for conveying feedback in a learning-oriented relationship. As participants exhibit diverse needs, interests, or preferences, the alignment of feedback mobilization techniques is necessary to maximize receptivity and application. A mentor can either explain salient lessons in explicit terms or facilitate introspection through open-ended questioning to construct insights. To cultivate intellectual capacity or healthy workplace culture, a blend of positive reaffirmation and constructive suggestions can be implemented in a feedback process. Although many developmental conversations may proceed positively, participants should be prepared to navigate difficult situations. The ability to denote challenges and explore divergent viewpoints can expand the sense-making process, but individuals must be respectful to maintain the relationship. The unique portfolio of skills, values, and characteristics can shape the interpretive lenses of collaborators in a learning connection. To convey messages in an appropriate and compelling manner, communicators must think critically about structures, word choice, tone, and body language elements. An improved self-awareness can influence the adjustment of behaviors to ensure that intention corresponds with impact. The recognition about equity, timeliness, or consistency can guide the distribution of standardization and individualization. Through effective multimodal feedback, participants can process best practices at a deeper level.

DOI: 10.4324/9781032715247-9

The guiding questions prompt evaluation of existing feedback processes and motivate relationship participants to evolve approaches based on organizational needs. First, individuals should consider: What strategies or structures are necessary to offer meaningful feedback, and why? A feedback exchange can transpire spontaneously and conclude within a few moments or represent a planned dialogue throughout an extended temporal horizon. For both scenarios, the possibility to impart revolutionary best practices can exist. The alignment of thoughtful feedback at the ideal time can reorient an individual toward co-constructed developmental goals. The meaningful component suggests that communicators should purposefully deliver insights to spark processing for counterparts. An aptitude to identify and vary strategies as appropriate can stimulate growth for relationship participants. The purpose may diverge based on circumstances such as emphasis on ideation or consolidation. As individuals may possess unique heuristics, a collaborative discussion about feedback structures can designate compelling frames. Second, practitioners should consider: What are organizational priorities for feedback type, and why? The relationship and program objectives can distinguish salient factors for information content and facilitation mode. If an initiative focuses on intellectual capacity, the conveyed feedback may allocate attention to technical or specialized task components. If an intervention emphasizes fostering of healthy workplace culture, the disseminated insights may delve into behavioral and relationship aspects. A program administrator should ponder whether the organizational and connection priorities are synergistic, which can be explored in initiation and planning phases. If participants are equipped with a feedback toolkit, learning dialogue can enhance development.

Feedback Platforms

An understanding about the feedback landscape can influence selections of the timing and location for best practice exchange. First, the verbal approach invites individuals to speak through in-person or virtual modalities to convey relevant information. For instance, a new front-line employee could receive positive and constructive comments after a shift about performance with an unfamiliar task. A verbal platform blends textual, visual, and auditory sources to guide the sense-making activities. The textual element is relevant as individuals may read and write ideas before a conversation to guide the language selection or phrasing. The visual standpoint is applicable since non-verbal cues of body language, facial expressions, distancing, or eye contact could complement the expressed sentiments. The auditory perspective is evident as individuals consider the aggregation of sounds through tone and pacing to interpret implicit themes. An advantage of verbal feedback is the opportunity to address misinterpretations or confusion in an immediate manner. Although preparation is helpful to influence effective delivery, the verbal nature can be less time-consuming as speaking may be quicker than writing. A disadvantage is individuals may decide to avoid critical feedback concerns depending on live reactions of their counterparts. As a result of technological advancements, the verbal method could occur through synchronous or asynchronous options to maximize accessibility based on individual preferences.

Second, the written approach permits individuals to explicitly present information through a hardcopy or electronic source. For example, a peer mentor in the educational sector could record observations about mentee teaching effectiveness in a report format. The written strategy leverages textual and visual factors but does not integrate an auditory source. A textual component is integral as individuals deliberately identify language, sentence framing, and paragraph structure to illustrate narratives. The visual area could be adopted if communicators highlight keywords, implement designs, and embed complementary images. An advantage for written feedback is the capability to review and revise information before distribution to the relationship collaborator. A disadvantage is the possibility for recipients to misinterpret the messaging based on the implemented textual and visual features. If a verbal conferencing opportunity does not occur, individuals may need to clarify feedback through additional written dialogue. The awareness about relationship needs can influence appropriate platform selection (Figure 8.1).

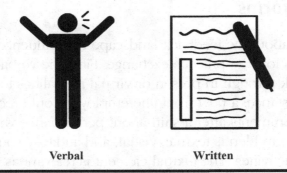

Verbal   **Written**

Figure 8.1   An overview of feedback platforms. (Developed by Amelia Knop.)

Feedback Process and Considerations

The explanation of possible feedback stages can generate clarity about execution of best practice exchange conversations. After the relationship participants co-construct learning goals and growth activities, the mentor can compile information from viewing, interactional, and output sources. At the appropriate debriefing phase, the mentor can start the conversation with a question or comment. If the mentor intends to spark introspection and invite counterpart viewpoints, an open-ended question can be posed for the response. An alternative is for the mentor to articulate facts or perceptions from the intervention and permit mentees to respond. The adopted strategy may depend on the relationship norms, learning preferences, or activity focus. For both the question and comment scenarios, the mentee subsequently has opportunities to convey insights. The mentee could decide to explain perspectives, pose clarification questions, or select a blended approach. A dialogue could continue until a discussion topic is exhausted or a time constraint is fulfilled. The extension of a conversation would involve pivoted dialogue between participants, where directive or facilitative techniques are appropriately identified.

An outline of feedback exchange considerations can influence individuals to think about the giving and receiving informational stages. First, feedback should be distributed in a delicate manner to appreciate diverse visible and invisible identities of members. Second, a thoughtful approach requires careful planning and introspection about the likely perceived impact for the counterpart. Third, processing time should be embedded so that individuals can engage in sense-making and respond authentically to best practice themes. Fourth, the orientation should be aspirational, as collaborators can embrace and use non-evaluative feedback about development. Fifth, questions and comments should be designed with an application lens so participants can implement lessons learned in cross-curricular contexts. The specified elements can serve as guiding criteria for preparation and dissemination of feedback. As individuals will offer best practices in a divergent manner, the commonalities can provide an overarching model. A comprehension about mentorship roles and responsibilities is critical for feedback framing (Figure 8.2).

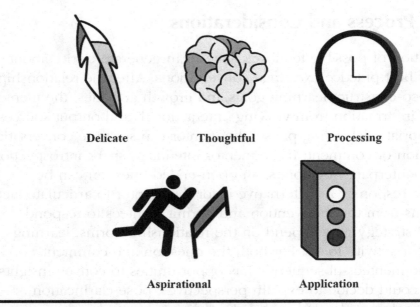

Delicate   **Thoughtful**   **Processing**

Aspirational   **Application**

Figure 8.2   An overview of feedback considerations. (Developed by Amelia Knop.)

Positive Reinforcement and Constructive Recommendation Pillars

Although feedback should be presented in an aspirational manner and leverage participant strengths, both positive and constructive pillars are still needed to facilitate development. First, positive reinforcement represents feedback that recognizes and encourages continuation of ideal task or relationship behaviors. For instance, a mentee who voluntarily remains at work after hours to share skills with a colleague who is struggling for an unfamiliar task deserves appreciation. The identified activity supports the cultivation of intellectual capacity and healthy workplace culture, so tailored recognition can motivate repetition of actions. The strategic communication of positive feedback is important to maintain value in the sentiments. If positive feedback is offered for every action, a recipient may perceive comments as disingenuous or exhibit confusion about the definition of exemplary behaviors. The absence of positive feedback can prompt counterpart thinking about whether the organization acknowledges and respects the conducted activities. A recommendation is to integrate at least one positive element into each session, while individualizing comments to distinguish value-added behaviors.

Second, constructive recommendation represents the articulation of approaches to improve achievement in task or relationship areas. For example, a mentee who does not review work products for word choice, phrasing, and structure could brainstorm strategies with a mentor to improve output quality. An alternative situation could be providing guidance to a mentee who consistently initiates conflict with a subordinate due to insecurity. The illustrated scenarios could hinder organizational performance or collaboration, so feedback should be disseminated to address the shortfalls. The wording, tone, and non-verbal behaviors for constructive comments are essential to consider, as individuals may exhibit lower receptivity to perceived criticism. A mentor can strategically navigate the situation through building rapport, reserving judgment, posing questions, and co-constructing next steps. If constructive feedback is provided for every behavior, individuals may become disengaged, frustrated, or disruptive. A prioritization of developmental areas can focus comments on critical areas to resolve for the interim. The absence of suggestions can be detrimental if unideal phenomena occur as a counterpart may deem the actions to be appropriate, especially if the mentor ignores the behavior. A mentor is not expected to resolve an emergency or extreme situation independently, as involvement of program coordinators may be necessary based on policy. An effective relationship or program should prioritize a lifelong learning environment to embrace feedback and apply strategies.

Navigation of Difficult Conversations or Conflicts

As mentorship participants exhibit diverse knowledge, skills, and experiences, conflicts may naturally emerge during feedback sessions. A healthy conflict seeks to explore divergence in perceptions or experiences to construct novel best practices for prospective implementation. However, an unhealthy disagreement could occur where individuals may express unprofessional comments, criticize people instead of ideas, or refuse acceptance about growth opportunities. The conflict could be initiated due to mentor or mentee behaviors, but attributing blame is less important in the moment than determining a positive resolution. To prepare participants for possible conflict, program administrators could implement case studies or role-play exercises in the onboarding session. The successful navigation of conflict could strengthen a connection based on conveyed character in the process. In contrast, unsuccessful mitigation could damage a relationship permanently based on the lack of consideration for individual feelings and needs.

To facilitate a difficult conversation or address conflict, participants should leverage interpersonal communication strategies. First, relationship collaborators should brainstorm and establish norms about approaches to appropriately respond in situations with tension. The explicit techniques can ensure shared understanding in advance of a challenging situation. Second, individuals should focus on concrete facts to minimize subjectivity in sense-making of topics. The synthesis of viewing, interactional, and output sources can compile available details. Third, members should ask open-ended questions to extract viewpoints and respectfully clarify misinterpretation areas. The recap and agreement about salient insights can narrow the gap in pinpointed difficulties. Fourth, tactful selection of language can prevent escalation of dialogue. The avoidance of first and second person could reduce the possibility of assigning fault or sparking personal reactions. Fifth, identification of an appropriate conferencing modality can anticipate and address confusion. A conversation could occur through a live in-person or virtual format to ensure individuals have opportunities to clarify sentiments promptly. Sixth, participants could initiate a break to briefly reflect and compose thoughts as needed. The intention is to eliminate disruptive reactions within the moment and permit members to regroup. Seventh, a mediator or impartial third party could be invited to witness the dialogue. The representative should not assume a stance and instead emphasize the implementation of mutually agreed norms. A strategy portfolio could be tailored to the participant, but prior thinking could reframe difficult moments (Figure 8.3).

Feedback Delivery Techniques

The effective identification of approaches to facilitate feedback can reinforce the disseminated content within a conferencing session. First, word choice or linguistic conventions could shape how meaning is transmitted across organizational units. An examination of context-specific terminology is valuable to anticipate how counterparts may interpret information based on unique positionality. For instance, a relationship where the mentor and mentee are both from the same engineering department could mobilize industry-based jargon in discussions. However, the same language may be difficult for individuals to decipher if the mentor from engineering

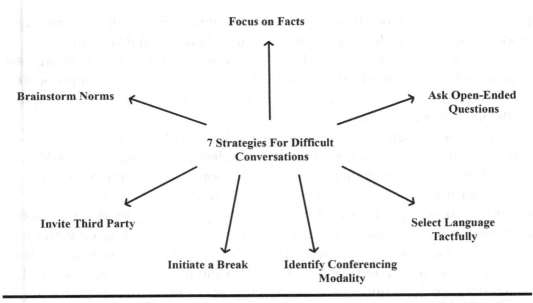

Figure 8.3   An overview of difficult conversation strategies. (Developed by Amelia Knop.)

is collaborating with a mentee from the medical sector. An additional consideration is how personal identities may influence the sense-making process. The age, gender, cultural background, language proficiency, educational level, and geographic location of an individual could intersect to influence how sentiments are interpreted. For example, a mentor who is participating in an international exchange program may be new to the region and learning the language. As a result, the selected terminology and framing may not communicate a message as initially intended. A conversation may not proceed perfectly, but using professional discretion to ensure any possible misinterpretation is minimal and not detrimental is critical to feedback.

Second, intonation, pacing, and conversation atmosphere may convey implied sentiments for participant processing. The purposeful variation in voice pitch could emphasize keywords or phrases within a discussion. A verbal avenue permits message communicators to reinforce and clarify resonating themes with articulation techniques. Through repeated interaction with a given individual, a counterpart can recognize baseline levels for expression. If a voice displays a higher intensity or volatility, the recipient may process the feedback with greater attention. A calmness in a voice may establish a relaxed environment to investigate next improvement steps with composure. The quickness or slowness of speech relative to typical behaviors could show anxiety or relaxation depending on personal tendencies. An individual should strategically align verbal features to message content. For instance, addressing a critical breach of professionalism requires a firm communication style to denote the severity. The appropriate use of voice can manage perceptions and impressions from counterparts to reaffirm themes in a clear manner.

Third, body language can exhibit factors for consideration through non-verbalized behaviors in a communication exchange. The elements could be deliberate if the individual controls the actions or unintentional if the participant naturally responds to organizational situations. A member should examine typical body language as viewpoints may be disseminated accidentally or inaccurately. For example, a mentee may not agree with the provided mentor's feedback and display frustration unconsciously through a facial disposition. The mentor could interpret the response as disrespectful, which may spark an unnecessary conflict. A series of movements such as changing positions or restlessness could signify processing or nervousness based on individual tendencies. A stretched-out stance could demonstrate control or comfort, while a closed posture may imply a lack of receptivity to expressed sentiments. The activation of hand gestures could capture individual emotions or provide visual cues for sense-making. As eye contact, relative spacing, and touch could differ across identities, participants should consider the counterpart behavior relative to average actions. Although word choice, tone, and body language could symbolize underlying insights in a feedback exchange, individuals must retain caution in developing assumptions. The collaborators could discuss observations to delve deeper into the conversation and reflect on personal behaviors to frame communication with intention (Figure 8.4).

| Word Choice | Intonation and Pacing | Body Language |

Figure 8.4 An overview of feedback delivery techniques. (Developed by Amelia Knop.)

Feedback Framing Structures

An overview of strategies to organize feedback can expand the mentorship toolkit for program participants during best practice exchanges. The structure can represent how sentiments are assembled, categorized, and examined in conferencing sessions. First, a directive mentor-initiated approach could communicate insights and permit mentee counterparts to respond. A mentor could record thoughts from available data sources to determine priorities based on the co-constructed learning outcomes. The relevant insights can subsequently be allocated to positive reinforcement and constructive recommendation classifications. Throughout the initiation phase, norm identification could involve dialogue about an appropriate ratio for positive to constructive feedback. As individual needs and preferences diverge, some participants may suggest less time for positive feedback to focus more comprehensively on improvement areas. If a feedback ratio is not specified, the communicator should consider a balance of positive and constructive based on learning intervention performance. The sequencing of feedback topics could similarly be investigated to determine whether positive or constructive comments should be illustrated first. A possible approach is to start and end with positive aspects, so the development areas are buffered. However, a later relationship stage or established rapport could influence individuals to adjust the order. A directive method still requires honest collaborative feedback to succeed.

Second, a facilitative mentee-driven method can embody an adaptive and unpredictable style where the feedback conversation flows naturally. The mentor could develop questions to generate introspection from the mentee, but the guiding prompts could start general and delve deeper as the participant shares perspectives. As the dialogue could proceed in an unexpected manner, the mentor navigator must identify compelling follow-up questions to capture salient learning outcomes. The exchange would invite the mentee to self-assess both positive and constructive areas, which can build reflective capacity for prospective learning interventions. Although the mentor may interpret the spiraled approach as unclear, the priority is for the mentee learner to become immersed in the developmental experience. The opportunity for the mentee to consolidate best practices at the conclusion of a thematic segment is necessary to ensure explicit understanding. An exploratory strategy could be implemented at any relationship stage, but the depth of shared perspectives may evolve as the connection solidifies. As mentorship involves repeated exchanges, participants could attempt both and vary between structures (Figure 8.5).

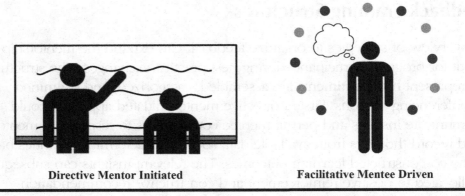

Directive Mentor Initiated   Facilitative Mentee Driven

Figure 8.5 An overview of feedback framing structures. (Developed by Amelia Knop.)

Feedback Communication Trade-offs

The investigation of feedback philosophies and implications for relative prioritization can guide individuals when strategies do not fully converge. First, a standardization method would align implemented activities with a specified threshold. For instance, a feedback standard could be to offer at least two constructive recommendations to a mentorship counterpart after each learning observation occurs. The content would differ across members and contexts, but the quantity of discussed topics could be uniformly maintained. Second, an individualization approach would tailor interventions based on differentiated factors for a given participant. For example, one mentee may prefer feedback through verbal and written modalities to maximize the sense-making process. Another mentee may ask for verbal feedback only due to literacy barriers with processing written sentiments. The mentor provides insights to the counterpart in both scenarios, but the modality diverges based on resonating needs for personalized development. As the standardization and individualization styles respectively entail uniformity and differentiation, the application to a single relationship facet could appear as mutually exclusive. However, both philosophies could be integrated within a mentorship relationship overall through diverse areas.

The equitable aspect considers perceptions of fairness about disseminated best practices within a mentorship program. Although individuals may assume that an equal amount and depth of feedback is critical, an equity mindset challenges stakeholders to investigate learner needs. As participants stem from unique identities, specific members may require additional support in designated domains. A standardization philosophy for feedback structure may preserve systemic barriers as the starting point in a growth journey is not necessarily identical. However, care for all mentorship counterparts could be standardized as a foundation for compassionate relations. An individualization approach could tailor goals, modalities, and language to each learner.

The timeliness element captures the potential turnaround speed for providing feedback to a mentorship participant. A verbal conferencing session may immediately offer commentary after a learning intervention since the communicator can articulate thoughts in the moment. The written feedback alternative could require additional time as individuals prepare, revise, and distribute the sentiments. The standardization of comments could accelerate feedback after the initial design time, but the information may be presented more generally. The individualization of sentiments could result in more time needed given the higher specificity, while the richness could be increased. As a result, time allocations could shape the depth of conveyed feedback.

The consistency component represents the similarity of thematic and structural pillars across mentorship conversations. As uniformity could transpire within content and delivery domains, individuals must think about both the messaging and facilitative behaviors. A standardization technique aligns with consistency as strategies are implemented as identically as possible across mentorship dyads. The individualization method generates inconsistency across connections as unique topics are discussed or instructional tactics are mobilized. Although the inconsistency may be perceived with a negative connotation, the specificity can be valuable for learner development. However, similarity in program stages can foster comparable experiences (Figure 8.6).

Standardization   Individualization

Figure 8.6   An overview of feedback methods. (Developed by Amelia Knop.)

Consolidation of Verbal and Written Feedback

The examination of feedback techniques across modalities can illuminate possibilities for best practice exchange. A communication style with delicate, thoughtful, reflective, aspirational, and practical aspects can ignite learning for program participants in positive or constructive areas. Conversations may exhibit diverse purposes, so reflection about structure, standardization, and individualization may guide facilitation or sense-making processes. As compiled feedback can highlight salient themes, a grasp of questioning techniques can extend stakeholder learning.

Chapter 9

Improve Engagement with Effective Questions

As a mentorship relationship intends to establish new and adjust existing best practices, the integration of meaningful questioning strategies can spark introspection. A connection can build over time as individuals cultivate understanding about appropriate norms. The introduction of collaborative inquiry can challenge individuals to think critically about progress and identify prospective actions. This chapter explores available questioning techniques for participants to generate engagement and deeper learning during the developmental process. A comparison of effective and ineffective questioning can illustrate considerations for the framing or delivery of guiding prompts. Through diversity in adopted approaches, facilitators can pinpoint salient perspectives, orient progress toward compelling goals, and consolidate supportive resources for sensemaking. The specification of open and closed question types can influence alignment with learning objectives, while language, timing, sequencing, and follow-up can expand the growth opportunity. A review of question samples can empower mentors and mentees to distinguish between descriptive and analytical pillars. As participants may possess unique motivations, interests, and openness levels, questions can be leveraged in the opening stage to formulate rapport or relevant insight about identity. The aptitude to pivot naturally between question themes and structures can illustrate entry points or impart perspective taking over time. Although questions may be quick to deliver, practice and refinement are necessary to maximize impact.

DOI: 10.4324/9781032715247-10

The guiding questions serve as possible examples to encourage dialogue from program stakeholders and invite ideation about applicable facilitation techniques. First, individuals should consider: How can questioning spark discussions about deeper situations, and why? A clear awareness about a question's purpose can ensure relevance to co-constructed learning goals. A developed question for one context may not be as compelling for an alternative environment. As a result, a precise understanding about the needs of learners is valuable. A general opening question could explore evident developmental themes, while a more specific sequencing of follow-ups can delve deeper into underlying phenomena. The question dissemination abilities should be complemented with active listening and critical thinking to generate an enriching discourse. The progression from recollection to evaluation could require facilitators to guide individuals through an iterative pathway of self-discovery. Second, practitioners should consider: How can content and style enhance receptivity to reflection, and why? A recognition of priority topics to investigate in a questioning session can ensure appropriate focus. The strategic links between guiding questions can improve interpretation, while highlighting actionable approaches for timely implementation. A thoughtful style can authentically integrate personal identity within conversation to provide psychological safety for honest expression. The learning environment can shape the willingness for individuals to demonstrate voice behaviors, share vulnerabilities, and self-assess progress. As a questioning journey promotes professional and personal ideation, relationship participants must allocate time, effort, and attention to achieve an optimal learning space. Each interaction can offer a reflective experience to improve questioning capacity.

Effective and Ineffective Questioning Techniques

The tailored preparation and implementation of effective questioning techniques can engage learners at diverse developmental stages. A successful question evolves from an anticipated growth outcome and has the potential to evoke metacognition through multimodal responses. Although a question may be designed appropriately for the learning context, an individual may not yet feel comfortable or equipped to respond with significant depth. As a result, the follow-up questions can proceed to pinpoint the current learning positionality. If a mentor aspires to identify best practices or factors, a direct question may be valuable to generate concrete answers. If a facilitator anticipates possible tension with a topic, an indirect question with delicate language may be ideal to offer a broader entry point. The specificity of prompts could be increased if a collaborator intends to contextualize essential elements within the experience. An exploratory approach could adopt a general framing where individuals may express viewpoints at a higher level and subsequently convey rationale to support sense-making. As the examination of effective questions involves numerous contingencies, the critical insight is that participants must leverage the available information at the time to determine framing. A retrospective review of posited questions may suggest revisions, but additional details become available in the aftermath. As a result, mentorship collaborators must prioritize respect and attentiveness in interactions to provide a platform for expression about counterpart narratives (Figure 9.1).

An ineffective question misaligns the requested information with the expressed learning intention or demonstrates carelessness for counterpart needs. As individuals will accumulate more information over time, the questioning scope should improve in a sequential manner. If a facilitator does not listen to responses or observe counterpart reactions, follow-up questions could infer a lack of awareness. A guiding prompt that unnecessarily or inappropriately probes sensitive topics could damage a learning landscape and constrain respondent openness. Although a

Effective Question

Figure 9.1   A depiction of an effective question. (Developed by Amelia Knop.)

posed question may be positively intentioned, the impact could still have negative implications for the participant. An effective questioning protocol could be compared to an algorithm, where communicators consistently mobilize new insights to improve the next iteration. The ineffective question label is not permanent, as individuals could pivot through appropriate vulnerability and willingness to process feedback. Through questioning experiences, individuals can cultivate the unique style and thematic portfolio that is necessary to influence development. An individual should think purposefully and creatively to maximize the long-term value of each question.

Importance of Variation in Questioning Strategies

As learning facilitators may adopt divergent approaches for posing questions, habits may emerge based on the interpreted success of implementation. The individual may develop an identity for asking questions and apply identical techniques across contexts. However, the participants should consider differentiation through refinement of strategies based on salient needs. A willingness to engage in variation practices can continue to evolve the living portfolio of best practices. If a method is perceived to be effective, replication could occur as the individual may not want to deviate and risk achieving fewer outcomes through additional experimentation. As a result, satisficing may transpire as the current options are deemed as acceptable. The mentor and mentee should instead be invited to attempt unique styles to recognize implications either through affirmation or negation. Affirmation can show that newly proposed techniques could extend or improve the current approach profile. In relation, negation could eliminate suggested methods based on viewing, interaction, and output sources. A collaborator should remember that boundary conditions could exist, so understanding the reasoning for generated impact is crucial to guide future decision-making. The variation between question compositions could stimulate participants intellectually, as routine expectations may prompt automated responses over time.

First, participants should diversify approaches to consolidate and verify resonating perspectives. If an individual consistently poses the same question type, respondents may express recurring viewpoints as the consequence of the prompt framing. The aptitude to pivot between question scope, language, and order can motivate counterparts to think holistically about the learning outcomes. Although a tendency may be to prioritize most frequently shared details, the appreciation for unique insights can identify alternative themes with possible significance. An exploratory orientation could support ideation about experiences, attitudes, and predictions. The confirmatory design could invite participants to convey relative agreement with themes, while denoting the sentiments as helpful or restrictive to goal achievement. A consolidation style could seek to summarize ideas for common understanding and position implications within the broader learning context. The verification method could ensure that respondents confirm the accuracy of the facilitator's interpretations about responses, which may guide the design of follow-up questions.

Second, individuals should vary questioning techniques to ensure appropriate learning trajectories based on relationship growth goals. For an initial conferencing session, members could engage in ideation about any resonating experiences and opportunities for development. The opening brainstorm can guide participants to co-construct learning objectives for upcoming activities and feedback exchanges. As the relationship progresses over time and anticipated benchmarks are communicated, the facilitator should ensure that questions extract applicable best practices. A segment could be allocated within conferencing for miscellaneous topics, but dedication to overarching goals is still needed. The dialogue about unrelated areas could spark ideation, while purposeful orientation can accelerate progress toward an ideal future state.

Third, rotated methods could accentuate learning gaps and influence participants to compile pertinent resources. Despite the perception that mentors are all-knowing individuals, the designated facilitators may encounter questions that spark development in unfamiliar areas. As a result, hardcopy and electronic materials could be mobilized for any program stakeholder to cultivate novel capacity. The encouragement of best practice exchange reinforces a healthy workplace culture of collaboration and social support, where needs can emerge through the questioning sessions. A framed inquiry could ask counterparts to explain professional and personal development interests, while a questioning set could evoke implicit awareness about priorities. To process, guide, and tailor learning, questions should leverage diverse designs (Figure 9.2).

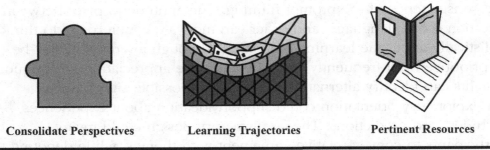

| Consolidate Perspectives | Learning Trajectories | Pertinent Resources |

Figure 9.2 An overview of question variation reasons. (Developed by Amelia Knop.)

Question Design Elements

The consideration of design components can guide facilitators about how to develop and revise effective questions. First, a description of open and closed ended question types can provide context about anticipated responses. An open-ended question represents an inquiry where individuals are encouraged to provide increased depth. The opportunity for elaboration exists as participants share supplementary details to support sense-making. For instance, a mentor could ask: Why do you hope to pursue positions of additional responsibility within the organization? The question could permit limitless permutations of answers from the mentee and provide autonomy to integrate resonating views within the dialogue. An advantage is participants could articulate personalized thoughts to offer a more comprehensive understanding about collaboratively identified topics. A disadvantage is that presented information can be overwhelming, so the facilitator may be unsure how to prioritize themes and proceed with subsequent questions. In contrast, a closed-ended question provides individuals with explicit or implicit alternatives to select. The narrower focus could offer specific insights in definitive terms, while demonstrating precision about expressed sentiments. For example, a mentor could posit: Are you happy with current relationships in the organization? The question prompts a yes or no response without any further commentary. An advantage is that conveyed insights can be clearly categorized and influence selection of subsequent questions. A disadvantage is participants may not have enough insight about underlying justification. The open-ended question type could be valuable as follow-up to a closed-ended question since a facilitator could delve deeper into initially expressed perspectives.

Second, exploration about language conventions at a word or question level can guide sense-making for the relationship collaborators. The word threshold signifies a single term which could be an emphasis area or combine with additional elements to formulate the theme. The awareness about words with similar but distinct meanings is important for specificity. For instance, a mentor could ask a mentee about engagement or participation. The intention may be to understand the mentee involvement in a learning intervention. Engagement could represent the attention to activities, whereas participation may denote the quantity and quality of contributions. The engagement term may exhibit less visibility than participation, so the selection of wording within the question could influence the feedback. In relation, the question threshold indicates the assembly of terms to encourage responses from counterparts. The ordering of the same words within a question can guide processing. For example, a mentor could ask: How are you progressing today? The mentor could alternatively posit: Today, how are you progressing? The preceding option could focus on the person, while the subsequent version may emphasize the timeframe. The punctuation could shape the delivery and verbal features may impact the interpretation stage. A word or question could have positive, negative, neutral, or ambivalent connotations.
As a result, individuals could seek feedback from diverse community stakeholders about the proposed language. The literacy facets could differ across identities, so participants must listen attentively to responses to gauge counterpart interpretation and pivot as needed. The presented answers do not need to match expectations but should relate to the learning outcome.

Third, an analysis of question timing and sequencing can influence the conversational environment to facilitate best practice exchange. The timing captures the position of a question during a learning session or within the relationship phases. An initial inquiry could be framed as an authentic well-being check-in to provide an opportunity for sharing about experiences. The following questions could investigate the co-constructed learning goals once a positive landscape is established. If a mentee has encountered challenging moments in a learning activity, a question to probe improvement areas may be better suited for a later session. The emotional or sensitive nature of some situations may require additional processing time. As a result, attention to verbal and non-verbal cues from the counterpart could spark adaptation in a questioning protocol. In contrast, a mentor could pose follow-up questions to delve deeper if

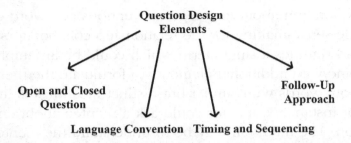

Figure 9.3   An overview of question design elements. (Developed by Amelia Knop.)

the mentee collaborator expresses openness at the moment. The amount of time since the discussed phenomena could influence the recall or metacognition of lessons learned. As time elapses, individuals may not remember minor details which are critical to the developmental process. However, debriefing immediately after an intervention may prompt too much focus on present priority areas. The relationship can evolve over time as individuals learn more about their counterparts. A delicate or intensive question could be applicable for later in the connection after rapport is established. An introductory prompt about identities could be tactfully conveyed at earlier stages to encourage exchanges. A cognizance about temporal horizons can anticipate receptivity and responsiveness (Figure 9.3).

Fourth, ideation about follow-up approaches can illuminate how to extract insights through additional inquiries. A follow-up can represent a question that continues with an identified learning theme. The clarification style offers a supplementary question to confirm understanding if any possible confusion or ambiguity remains. If a mentor asks a mentee about positive experiences in a team but the mentee focuses on negative situations, the mentor could probe whether any positive elements could be recalled. The mentee may have misunderstood the overall theme or diverted attention to another resonating area. An extension style intends to delve deeper into shared sentiments or pinpoint thoughts more specifically for a topic. If a mentee responds to an initial inquiry about motivational factors, the mentor could ask about the relative prioritization or reasoning for selection. The clarification and extension follow-up questions can be implemented until unified interpretation or insight repetition occurs, respectively. The question types, language, timing, and follow-up can collectively influence the dialogue richness (Figure 9.4).

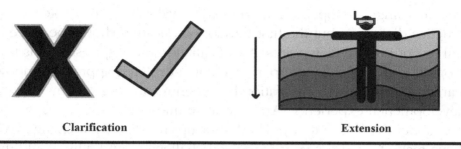

Clarification   Extension

Figure 9.4 An overview of follow-up approach styles. (Developed by Amelia Knop.)

Question Samples

To synthesize lessons learned about effective design, example questions
will be reviewed with commentary about strength and improvement
areas. First, sample prompts are examined from a broader organizational
context for a newly hired employee. An opening question could be: What
inspired or motivated you to join the organization, and why? The closed
elements can invite a counterpart to identify the main reasons for pursuing
the new position. The open-ended option permits individuals to expand
on professional and personal identities to offer context. Any initially
compiled insights can provide a foundation for dialogue during the learning
relationship. A subsequent question may be: What specific developmental
goals do you aspire to achieve through your participation in the mentorship
program, and why? The inquiry can encourage an individual to engage in
reflection about relevant success criteria with significance. However, the
question could possibly be reframed: What specific knowledge, skills, and
experiences do you intend to develop during the mentorship program, and
why? The three learning categories could be divided into separate questions
for clarity, while the increased precision can narrow the scope. The inclusion
of explanation opportunities could disseminate supplementary insights to
guide the facilitator in sequential question framing. The follow-up question
could be: Which of the presented goals is most important to you, and why?
Although an intention may be to achieve as many objectives as possible, the
prioritization could showcase member interests and preferences.

Second, example questions are evaluated in the context of a learning
intervention debriefing. For instance, an experienced teacher may be
delivering a lesson to students with observation from a peer mentor. The
mentor could posit: How could using a pair-share strategy more effectively

promote learning? The open-ended framing is valuable to promote constructive discourse, but the first developed question should be more general to not impose viewpoints. As a facilitator, the responsibility is to spark metacognition from the counterpart. A mentee-centered approach empowers the learner to orient the conversation based on resonating sentiments from the developmental experience. An alternative question could be: How did you feel about the lesson today? The follow-up may be: What changes could you have made to address your expressed challenges, and why would the strategies be effective? The opening inquiry serves as a well-being check-in as the mentee could express perceptions about content, delivery, or personal characteristics. If the mentee shares some constructive areas, the follow-up is appropriate to prompt thinking about recommendations while gradually becoming more specific. As a result, the progression of questioning themes with consideration for prior responses is critical.

Third, exemplar probes can influence individuals to think critically about adopted phrasing. For example, a mentor may attempt to navigate a difficult conversation with a mentee who escalated conflict with a dissatisfied customer. A possible question could be: Why did you unnecessarily make comments to deliberately anger a customer? The second-person language positions the individual directly within the situation and could generate defensive reactions, which differs from the non-evaluative growth goal. The terms of unnecessarily and deliberately represent assumptions about the counterpart's behaviors or intentions. As a result, the mentor should instead adopt delicate framing and permit the mentee to share perspectives in a productive manner. An alternative opening question could be: Can you please share your thoughts about the experience with the angry customer today? The sharing language invites the mentee to engage in a learning dialogue with the mentor, while the integration of essential facts provides enough direction for the discussion. The follow-up questions could leverage the illustrated details to learn more about the participant experience and co-construct best practices for future action. A sample question exercise could be implemented to investigate topics within a specific context (Figure 9.5).

Why did you unnecessarily make comments *to deliberately anger a customer?*

Can you please share your thoughts about the *experience with the angry customer today?*

Figure 9.5   A sample question comparison. (Developed by Amelia Knop.)

Questioning Implications for Unique Participant Entry Points

As individuals may participate in a mentorship program for diverse reasons, an appreciation for the entry point is necessary to create effective questions. A mentor could be required to provide organizational service, which may prompt involvement, while the same position could instead be adopted due to interest in supporting the community. A mentee could embark on a mentorship journey as part of mandatory positional requirements, but the learner could alternatively volunteer to build capacity. A wide variety of participation conditions may emerge for both mentors and mentees, so questioning techniques grounded in learner needs can similarly cultivate development. If program admission requirements are evident, the mentor and mentee should demonstrate awareness about the inclination for involvement. However, the presence of ambiguous engagement factors could spark an initial questioning stream. A member could ask: What motivated you to join the mentorship program, and why? The justifications could illustrate whether an individual has positive, negative, neutral, or ambivalent thoughts about program participation. If positive sentiments are expressed, the counterpart could reinforce the engagement with follow-up questions about the theme. If negative insights are conveyed, the counterpart could ask: How can we identify and implement strategies to maximize the value of our collaboration in the mentorship relationship? The framing encourages the participants to specify possible best practices, while permitting openness to discuss hesitations or perceptions. The initial questions and corresponding responses could be mobilized strategically to build a solid foundation. Although some individuals may not originally view the forthcoming experience to be meaningful, each discussion topic has the possibility to ignite counterpart engagement (Figure 9.6).

A commitment to authenticity and trust within the mentorship process could establish a platform for enriching dialogue. The investigation of intrinsic and extrinsic motivators could denote strategies to enhance effort within the learning journey. For example, an individual could ask: What approaches have motivated you to succeed in past professional learning activities? As members may not have participated before in a formal mentorship program, the activity framing could ignite self-reflection about developmental strategies. An exploration of personal interests may identify possible convergence areas to facilitate initial perspective-taking.

Unique Participant Entry Points

Figure 9.6   A depiction of unique entry points. (Developed by Amelia Knop.)

A counterpart could posit: What interests do you have beyond your professional position, and why? The hobbies and affiliations can provide baseline details about identities, while the open-ended framing can permit individuals to share information based on comfort levels. As values can influence behaviors and decision-making, opening prompts about the authentic state could showcase guiding principles. A member could ask: How would you describe yourself in a sentence to others, and why? The concise depiction could exhibit how an individual views the self and offer a preliminary preview about strength areas to leverage. The trust domain can be pinpointed explicitly through direct questions or implicitly through general conversation. A collaborator could posit: What techniques have strengthened your past or current relationships in learning contexts? Although an individual may want to ask about past challenges to identify lessons, negative framing could disrupt rapport, so positive orientations should be prioritized.

Consolidation of Improve Engagement with Effective Questions

Through an examination about appropriate questioning strategies, mentorship program participants can extract relevant information from dialogue for enhanced learning. A variation in question types, language, timing, sequencing, and follow-up frames can stimulate individuals to share novel best practices. The use of an ineffective question is inevitable but valuable to the developmental process, so collaborators must aggregate insights to appropriately pivot. As diverse mentorship topics have been explored, success factor synthesis can guide program assessment.

Chapter 10

Self-Assessment Scorecard

A compilation of illustrated themes for mentorship relationships and programs provides the cognitive foundation to establish a scorecard to self-assess achievement. Although a learning journey may proceed as a non-linear trajectory, synthesis of overarching progress is still critical to determine the generated value. The encountered growth can shape both the professional and personal domains, which have the potential to transform organizational phenomena. This chapter demonstrates a balanced scorecard approach for the evaluation of goal achievement, where the suggested general criteria can be tailored specifically to a learning context. As each team, department, institution, or community can exhibit diverse priorities, the intention of a sample scorecard is to spark metacognition about organized structures for gauging success. A mentorship exchange does not evaluate participants as people, but instead considers the task and relationship areas to diagnose the next steps for improvement. The self-assessment activity could occur formally or informally as an ongoing opportunity to think critically or creatively about recommendations. The integration of start, continue, and stop framing can clearly articulate lessons learned for the mentor, mentee, program administrator, and broader community stakeholders. The insights will diverge across participant identities based on unique values, philosophies, and aspirations. A mentee-centered style invites the individual to assemble and showcase evidence in the reflection conferences while recording best practices for possible future reference as a lifelong learner.

The guiding questions prompt reflective organizations to pinpoint salient strategies for analysis and co-construct compelling discourse topics to

DOI: 10.4324/9781032715247-11

structure assessment. First, individuals should consider: How can a balanced scorecard incentivize authentic learning and appropriate risk-taking, and why? The balanced consideration reminds participants that multiple success criteria are embedded in an intervention and learning occurs from numerous developmental domains. An ideation session about pertinent criteria can prompt relative prioritization to include the most important elements within the introspection model. The scorecard framing encourages stakeholders to determine appropriate quantitative and qualitative evidence to support the sense-making process. Through data from viewing, interaction, and output sources, individuals can evaluate similarities or differences to capture learning gaps. The commitment to authenticity requires that both participants in a dyad have autonomy to share perceptions as a bidirectional exchange. If an individual becomes preoccupied with percentage scores, appropriate risk-taking may be diminished. As a result, categorization of below, meets, and exceeds can alleviate stress. Second, practitioners should consider: What organization-specific categories should be included within the scorecard, and why? The presented template is developed generally as a starting point for implementation in any learning organization. However, improving meaning generation can stem from a willingness to tailor a framework to context-specific needs or phenomena. The strategic activation of multimodal avenues to compile insights from diverse stakeholder identities is valuable to navigate possible biases from homogeneous discussion. A scorecard could serve as a living artifact where adaptations are implemented over time based on evolving organizational complexities. The mechanism could encompass segments from unique organizational units so that criteria effectively capture emphasis areas from the micro, meso, and macro levels.

Reasons to Establish a Progress Assessment Framework

The motivation to consolidate best practices can influence participants to develop and implement an assessment framework. A collaboratively established structure can organize themes more clearly to spark the evaluation and recommendation processes. The rationale for adopting the assessment model occurs in both relationship and program contexts. A relationship landscape captures implications directly through an empirical lens. First, the scorecard offers a relevant resource to guide self-assessment of mentor and mentee needs. If the learner does not fulfill specified objectives, the participants can discuss possible causes and co-construct an action plan to demonstrate higher levels of achievement. The absence of a scorecard could influence the individuals to estimate progress without compelling evidence, while possibly offering ineffective positive or constructive feedback. Second, the framework can be leveraged as a formative gauge for progress during initiation and ongoing stages. An individual may quickly exceed standards in one category but unexpectedly perform below expectations in an alternative criterion. The compiled data can inform participants about necessary pivots for strategy in a timely manner. Third, the model can ensure orientation in program activities to maximize growth in resonating pillars. The construction phase can prompt discussion about how identified resources, activities, and pathways could satisfy achievement while synergizing decisions to promote learning (Figure 10.1).

The program threshold invites participants to consider how lessons learned can influence organizational activities. First, mentorship initiatives should align elements between relationship and organization standpoints for optimal return on investment. If the relationship aspirations are completely distinct from the organizational mission, vision, and values, the benefits may not apply to relevant institutional needs. As a result, organizational templates can provide criteria for at least some elements of the resource. Second, adoption of common framework components can permit comparison of learning objectives across dyads. The best practices can shape relationship design for prospective iterations while recognizing any possible antecedents for optimal learning conditions. Third, aggregated data from the program can influence the formulation of tailored training resources. A standardized approach to professional and personal development beyond a program may

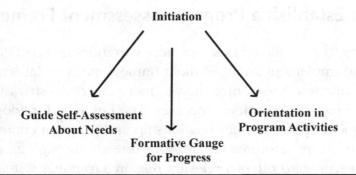

Figure 10.1 A summary of relationship-based initiation reasons. (Developed by Amelia Knop.)

not generate engagement or maximize learning. The compiled insights can guide decisions to impact participants as positively as possible from task and relationship areas.

Balanced Scorecard Components Overview

The description of common elements within a balanced scorecard can guide program stakeholders about how to adapt the general version to the specific organization. First, the resource should offer three to five overarching criteria for assessment. The criteria should be co-constructed based on prioritized relationship and initiative goals, while a range is articulated since the required time for an objective could differ. The minimum threshold is suggested so that learners focus on multiple and possibly complementary learning areas in the developmental activities. A maximum threshold is recommended so that too many facets are not explored, which could overwhelm the participants and reduce the depth of growth in a category. A weighting out of 100 percent for each criterion could be determined to showcase the relative value based on devoted time or individualized need level. The approach is not mandatory but could apply if a program adopts a common template and relationships have divergent starting points. Second, an explanation of the criteria including learning activities, resources, timeframes, and milestones could generate clarity for participants. The outline could evolve over time based on experiences and reflections, but the description is valuable to co-construct an evident progress plan. Third, specification of success indicators for below, meet, or exceed standard levels could be integrated. A tendency may be to focus on quantitative criteria only, as measurability may be simpler, but qualitative metrics are similarly important to capture narratives from the learning journey. Although content will differ, the three expressed components can be used across scorecards (Figure 10.2).

Possible Criterion 1: Intellectual Capacity through Knowledge, Skills, and Experiences

A first examined criterion captures intellectual capacity and the ability to mobilize cognitive resources to improve performance within organizational tasks. The achievement could blend the three sub-elements of knowledge,

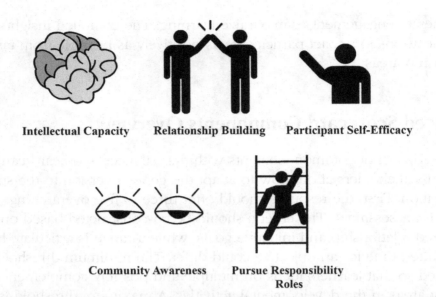

Intellectual Capacity   Relationship Building   Participant Self-Efficacy

Community Awareness   Pursue Responsibility
Roles

Figure 10.2   A sample of possible balanced scorecard criteria. (Developed by Amelia Knop.)

skills, and experiences. First, the accumulation of novel insights from general and specific contexts can influence processing of phenomena. The knowledge extension process could involve discussion with experienced individuals, review of theoretical or practical materials, and participation in debriefing sessions. Second, the enhanced or refined capability to effectively complete selected activities can guide execution. The skill development process could include engagement in learning activities, repetition with feedback from a counterpart, and experimentation with self-evaluation. Third, exposure to unique events or situations can prompt metacognition about stakeholder identities and organizational processes. The experiential exploration could encompass viewing of institutional activities, interaction with diverse participants, and participation in exercises. The criterion synthesizes the three intellectual capacity influences to build capacity for positive contributions to tasks in the project portfolio (Figure 10.3).

Although the generalized criterion appears abstract, the language can be explicitly tailored to the relationship and program intentions. For instance, an individual could articulate the objective as assembling enough applicable knowledge to successfully complete an industry-specific designation exam. An individualized benefit may be the ability to offer novel insights within

Knowledge   Skill   Experience

Figure 10.3   An overview of intellectual capacity sub-elements. (Developed by Amelia Knop.)

projects based on the uniquely compiled knowledge. The organizational implication could be new perspectives for improved work products, which could prompt referral to new clients. The learning activities may involve conceptual seminars, practice tests, and debriefing with an experienced mentor who has earned the designation within the past couple of years. A relevant resource portfolio could involve release time, learning guides, office space, and testing software. The timeframe could be completion within the next six months, while milestones may entail passing level achievement on at least three practice tests before the official exam session. To disseminate insights, the mentee could subsequently participate as a mentor for future candidates. As a result, the intellectual capacity can have implications for the participant and institution.

Possible Criterion 2: Relationship Building to Cultivate Healthy Workplace Culture

A second investigated criterion prioritizes a workplace culture grounded in collaboration, constructive dialogue, and social support through appropriate relationship-building activities. The development of a best practice exchange network considers the quality, quantity, and diversity of connections within an organizational ecosystem. First, a quality relationship can signify an interaction with mutual respect, openness, and engagement. As the connection may require time to flourish, participants should ask open-ended questions, co-construct norms, and acknowledge successes. Second, the quantity viewpoint reinforces the importance of initiating dialogue with

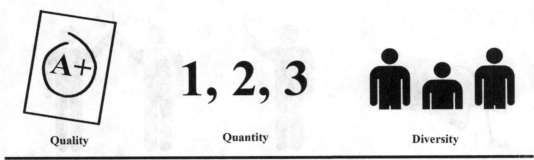

Figure 10.4   An overview of relationship-building considerations. (Developed by Amelia Knop.)

multiple individuals. If a member has limited relationships or refuses to connect with others, the opportunity to transmit insights and collaboratively identify interventions can be missed. Third, the diversity standpoint encourages individuals to cultivate links across identities or organization units. The heterogeneity could prompt constructive discourse necessary for continued growth (Figure 10.4).

The articulation of a specific mentorship instance can demonstrate how to apply the criterion within an institution. For example, a mentee in the financial department may aspire to improve efficiency of processes but hopes to leverage stakeholder feedback. The professional implication could be enhanced effectiveness in decision-making through insights from unique positionalities. A personal benefit could be new friendships within the organization to improve belongingness and well-being. The learning activities could be mentor introductions to possible collaborators, guidance about formal outreach, or initiation of cross-departmental sessions. The resources may involve meeting locations or subsidies for team building, while a timeframe could be within the next quarter. The milestones could entail at least ten new relationships with monthly interaction and representation from multiple departments. A longitudinal analysis of 360-degree feedback and tracking of interactions could be compared to subsequent organizational outputs.

Possible Criterion 3: Participant Self-Efficacy to Achieve High Standards

A third pinpointed criterion emphasizes the empowerment of learners to generate belief in the ability to continue improving and pursuing ambitious objectives. As individuals possess unique characteristics, philosophies, and motivators, sense-making strategies may differ. A participant could have high levels of confidence and adaptability to overcome adversities in a learning journey. Although the elements may be framed positively, the individual may need guidance about how to identify improvement areas and determine compelling areas to invest their time. In contrast, another member may consistently doubt decision-making and require extended time to evaluate alternatives. The commitment to metacognition may be valuable to avoid any reckless selections, but the indecisiveness may significantly delay progress. As a result, the learners could require a balance between perseverance, resourcefulness, and patience. A mentor could facilitate awareness while navigating reinforcement and discourse to build self-efficacy.

The specification of a sample scenario can illustrate the importance of sparking belief from both task completion and relationship development areas. For instance, a mentor could conference with a mentee to uncover insecurities and co-construct strategies to leverage personalized strengths. An individual benefit could be self-fulfillment of higher-level goals to pursue unprecedented outcomes, while the organizational implication could be continued improvement of standards. The learning activities could include mentee reflections with mentor questioning techniques and development of a strengths map to showcase unique abilities. The required resources could include independent locations, manipulatives, software, and grants to encourage goal pursuit. The milestones may be self-reported changes in belief, identification of novel achievements, and analysis of personal goal completion. The dedication to fostering self-actualization could serve as a catalyst for individuals to embark on a new achievement threshold.

Possible Criterion 4: Synthesis of New Perspectives to Evoke Community Awareness

A fourth highlighted criterion prioritizes improved understanding of stakeholder needs from the broader community. As individuals in an organization may exhibit privilege, purposeful actions to compile diverse viewpoints can enhance sense-making and decision-making. The attention to unique perspectives can spark awareness about how to challenge existing structures or assumptions for enhanced accessibility. The second criterion positions the learner within the relationship to directly benefit the participant and counterparts. In contrast, the depicted fourth criterion invites the possibility of cultivating both direct and indirect impact within the community through transformative change. The mentor and mentee should remember that the frequency of expressed insights is not the most important factor as alternative viewpoints still require consideration. An ongoing dialogue in a developmental relationship can encourage ideation for actionable strategies and influence communication techniques about resonating themes.

The introduction of a possible learning situation could reinforce the value of compiling best practices from diverse community collaborators. For example, a mentor could guide a mentee through the process of identifying assumptions, investigating sources, and recognizing implications for task or relationship behaviors. The individual ramifications could ignite awareness about unfamiliar areas that require additional exploration. An organizational benefit could be initiative of participants to invite perspectives from unique individuals to remove performance and collaboration barriers. The learning activities could entail a current perceptions inventory, an open-ended questioning session, and an organizational artifact review. The resources could be note-taking templates, diverse literature, and release time. As an ongoing intervention, the milestones may be specification of at least one organizational action project or participation in collaborative inquiry. The underlying intention is to spark authentic community connectivity.

Possible Criterion 5: Preparedness to Pursue Additional Responsibility Roles

A fifth explored criterion could depend on the salient signals for the initiation of a mentorship program. The options may include an expanded customer base, improved retention of members, recruitment of specialty skillsets, and facilitation of professional development for community stakeholders. The criterion could vary across individual positions, department affiliations, and industry dynamics. The differentiated design is implemented to encourage development in a relevant domain. A suggested pillar is accumulating necessary competency to transition into roles of additional responsibility within the organization. Although every individual may not be interested in advancement, the cultivated abilities could still enhance effectiveness within the current positionality. An evaluation of a prospective position description could pinpoint growth areas, while discussion with individuals in the role could uncover the unwritten elements. The internal promotion of candidates could sustain a positive culture.

The illustration of a positional trajectory in an organization with a hierarchical structure could provide clarity about how to influence preparedness. For instance, a mentor could invite a mentee counterpart to develop a candidate profile for positions of additional responsibility. The specification of competencies and emergent gaps could influence an action plan for growth. An individual benefit could be the acquisition of qualifications and refinement of abilities to one day progress in the organizational pathway. An institutional implication may be the initiation of a positional pipeline to address openings in a timely and effective manner. The learning activities could be accreditation program registration, committee participation, and discernment sessions. The resources could include grants, release time, connections, office space, and infrastructure, while the timeframe could be in the next year. The milestone could be progressive achievement of mandatory position prerequisites, while the learner could assemble a best practice portfolio.

Scorecard Development Guiding Questions

As the proposed scorecard template offers general themes, program administrators and participants should consider specific criteria within the co-construction process. A series of guiding questions can spark thinking about relevant priorities. The first prompt is: What concrete knowledge, skills, or experiences are most critical to expanding intellectual resources in the future, and why? As organizations consistently evolve, a prospective ideation about needs and gaps can influence selection of learning activities. A second question is: How could the environment be improved to encourage relationship-building for a healthier workplace culture? An understanding of tactics to foster connections through mentorship or beyond can increase the quality, quantity, and diversity of best practice exchange. A third inquiry is: What are low self-efficacy areas for the program participant, and why? An identification of current hesitation aspects could illuminate priorities for development and probe investigation of underlying causes. A fourth prompt is: To what extent are perspectives synthesized from diverse participants, and why? The intention is to think creatively about how to nurture a community of accessibility and collaboration. A fifth question is:

What individual and organizational need areas could align in a program, and why? A synergy between participant and institutional goals can evoke engagement in a learning journey.

Learning Plan Methodology

Through the use of the established scorecard for self and peer assessments, mentorship relationship participants can co-construct learning plans. The developmental actions can be identified and implemented at divergent temporal horizons. A framework could be adopted for a diagnostic assessment at the start of a program so that the learner can specify current proficiency in the categories. An initial discussion about why a below, meet, or exceed achievement level is selected can provide valuable insights for the ideation of learning activities. The model could be reviewed independently or collaboratively throughout the initiative tenure to denote progress. An awareness of present strengths and weaknesses can shape conferencing sessions or pursue developmental pathways. The resource could be leveraged at a summative or closing stage in the relationship to establish the next steps for the mentee. A mentor could continue to support the mentee if mutual agreement is expressed. As a result, a scorecard should be viewed as ongoing reference material. The clear and concise construction is critical to increase the likelihood of usage.

As discussions about progress based on the scorecard criteria could generate significant information, a suggested methodology for creating action plans could be integrated. A start, continue, and stop framing blends the strategies of positive reinforcement and constructive feedback to orient learning. First, a start recommendation represents an action to begin that was not previously adopted. For instance, a mentee could start allocating 30 minutes each day to initiate new relationships in the office. Second, a continue-oriented suggestion represents an action to sustain that has been implemented. The purpose is to create awareness and reaffirm appropriate behaviors. For example, a mentee could continue participating in a professional learning community to compile best practices. Third, a stop proposition represents an action to terminate that has been used before. For instance, a mentee could stop making negative comments about colleagues. The technique serves as a possibility for individuals to mobilize in the learning process, but identification of alternative strategies could be relevant based on member needs (Figure 10.5).

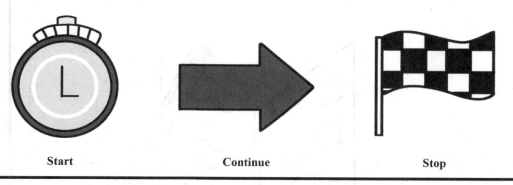

| Start | Continue | Stop |

Figure 10.5   A depiction of start, continue, and stop framing. (Developed by Amelia Knop.)

Growth Demonstration Using Evidence

The assessment scorecard seeks to ignite development from professional and personal standpoints, so participants should compile evidence to illustrate new best practices. For each of the co-constructed criteria, an individual can identify and display multimodal products to explain lessons learned. The integration of textual, visual, and auditory features can enhance reflection for relationship participants while personalizing the growth experience. A showcase opportunity could occur through conferencing sessions with mentors, presentations to community members, and discussions involving supervisors. The use of open-ended initial and follow-up questions can encourage learners to justify inclusion of evidence in the dialogue. Any personalized narratives can complement numerical metrics to capture growth in task and relationship domains. For example, an individual could consolidate certificates from professional learning modules and articulate salient developmental themes. An annotation approach could be activated where individuals record thoughts and feelings about materials using sticky notes. The learning activities may occur well before a debriefing session, so the documentation of perspectives can spark recollection and dialogue. To enrich the available evidence, individuals should leverage both quantitative and qualitative sources. For instance, a mentee could convey improvement in customer satisfaction scores and present the submitted testimonials. The numerical data can provide the possibility for trend analysis using statistical techniques, while the linguistic insights can encourage thematic coding. A demonstration of evidence is not intended as a busy work project but is instead designed to reinforce new lessons learned and disseminate insights to counterparts (Figure 10.6).

Figure 10.6   A depiction of a multimodal lessons learned portfolio. (Developed by Amelia Knop.)

Consolidation of Self-Assessment Scorecard

An introduction to self-assessment resources can invite program participants to gauge progress throughout a learning journey. The suggestion of possible criteria may prompt thinking about developmental goals, while learning activities, timeframes, and success indicators can establish clarity about the next steps. The development of action plans through tailored methodology can synthesize resonating areas and cultivate a personalized best practice portfolio. To share new insights with stakeholders, participants should pinpoint relevant products that display growth. The recommended scorecard criteria reinforce importance of equity, diversity, and inclusivity.

Chapter 11

Equity, Diversity, and Inclusivity in Mentorship

To cultivate intellectual capacity and healthy workplace culture through mentorship relationships, program stakeholders must consider how to maximize accessibility for learning opportunities. The purposeful implementation of strategies to address barriers across unique organizational units can maximize possibilities for professional and personal development. This chapter examines the pillars of equity, diversity, and inclusivity within a mentorship context to pinpoint suggestions for improved accessibility. As needs and identities will diverge across individuals, an environment of constructive discourse can illuminate tailored interventions to enhance learning trajectories. Although an idealistic approach is to eliminate all challenges immediately, change is an ongoing process of adaptation that requires openness and continued experimentation. The involvement of individuals from diverse visible and invisible identities in dialogue can highlight novel perspectives to leverage in decision-making. A landscape grounded in psychological safety and collaboration can continue to expand the portfolio of best practices through authentic expression. The program design may evolve based on a review of available data sources, while co-construction of differentiated implementation plans can generate engagement. The commitment to fairness, representation, and belongingness can maximize the lessons learned for any initiative participant. A courageous and vulnerable disposition is necessary for program administrators to acknowledge, brainstorm, and implement techniques focused on accessibility.

DOI: 10.4324/9781032715247-12

The guiding questions situate accessibility principles as foundational pillars within mentorship programs since growth can be accentuated with equity, diversity, and inclusivity. First, individuals should consider: What organizational equity, diversity, and inclusivity challenges limit mentorship effectiveness, and why? Identification of challenges requires critical and creative thinking as members must examine phenomena from unique perspectives. As individuals exhibit divergent heuristics, sense-making of the same situation may prompt variable reactions and insights. The available information can be overwhelming, so a mentorship landscape emphasizes introspection about relationship norms, learning activities, and program design. An equitable lens examines the fairness of interventions across people or contexts, where equality does not necessarily represent justice. The diversity view consolidates the representation of relationship or program participants from numerous visible and invisible identity domains. An inclusive standpoint investigates the perceived belongingness of community stakeholders as genuine collaborators in the developmental journey. Second, practitioners should consider: How can relationships with unique identities generate unprecedented learning, and why? Although a tendency may exist where individuals interact with counterparts from similar identities, value exists in best practice exchange with diverse representatives. A similar connection can reinforce existing assumptions, biases, or beliefs while providing comfort to proceed with development. However, a dissimilar link can naturally spark constructive discourse to explore phenomena from a novel positionality. The co-construction of norms is critical as conflict should be pursued respectfully, especially when individuals extend beyond their comfort zone to reconsider situations. If any relationship is nurtured effectively, a possibility exists for significant learning to emerge. As a result, a thoughtful review of learning conditions can generate ideation about accessibility.

Accessibility in the Mentorship Learning Process

A mentorship relationship is comprised of many smaller decisions which can collectively reinforce or constrain the overarching learning process. The aspiration to accumulate new best practices and encourage community-building behaviors can depend on the learning factors. An accessible mentorship relationship can represent a connection where participating organizational units have opportunities to achieve objectives. The identification of barriers can be simplistic for visible phenomena through viewing, interactional, and output sources. In contrast, underlying or invisible elements can require strategic techniques such as open-ended questioning. A limitation can transpire deliberately or unintentionally, while practices may be adopted recently or signify recurring activities. The opportunity for individuals to satisfy professional or personal potential can stem from both task and relationship elements. An insightful facilitation of relevant content in understandable terms based on learner needs may improve performance, while active listening could enhance rapport. Accessibility can leverage unique abilities to create enriching learning platforms for the individual, collaborators, and broader community. A relationship can pivot in a bidirectional manner between accessible and inaccessible status, so ongoing care is critical.

The accessibility challenges can emerge from human and non-human areas. First, the human viewpoint considers the behaviors of counterparts or administrators that shape learning outcomes. A lack of openness to mentor feedback can disrupt the developmental process as the adopted attitude may constrain rapport, perspective-taking, and constructive discourse. The inequitable allocation of time or effort across mentees could provide advantages to selected individuals and disadvantage alternative members. An absence of prerequisite knowledge, skills, and experiences could influence the ability to ask compelling questions or facilitate dialogue. Second, the non-human standpoint considers the financial, physical, and technological structures which can alter learning trajectories. The need to pursue additional employment opportunities could prevent individuals from participating if release time is not offered. A location without accommodated resources or layouts can limit individuals from engaging in learning activities. The lack of hardware and software could hinder involvement in a multimodal or virtual program structure. An ongoing attention to human and non-human factors can exhibit supportive or constraining aspects, so dialogue through diverse mentorship connections may ignite awareness (Figure 11.1).

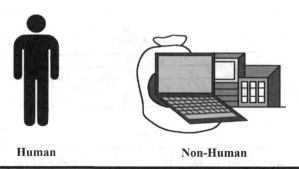

Human   Non-Human

Figure 11.1 **An overview of accessibility challenge areas. (Developed by Amelia Knop.)**

Recognizing Privilege and Supporting Marginalized Groups

An understanding of diverse participant positionalities can guide strategies to create and maintain dyadic learning opportunities. First, traditionally privileged individuals possess advantages which may expedite or accentuate accessibility within programs. The differentiation could stem from identities such as expressed gender, age, ethnicity, religion, sexual orientation, spoken languages, socio-economic status, social affiliations, educational level, professional background, or specialized education needs. The illustrated elements do not consolidate an exhaustive list, as a significant quantity of additional identities could be prevalent within diverse contexts. As individuals have a unique profile of intersecting identities, the areas of privilege may likely differ across the participants. A dominating area pinpoints an identity that could have possessed a higher advantage level consistently throughout history. For example, an individual who has a combination of male, older, Caucasian, Christian, heterosexual, English-speaking, financially wealthy, socially elite, university graduate, working professional, and high-ability identities could have privilege. If a participant authentically recognizes advantage sources, the privilege can be leveraged to address barriers, establish opportunities, and spark change. Personalized values and philosophy can shape how initiatives of equity, diversity, and inclusivity are activated. Although a perception could be that privileged individuals should retain benefits for the self, cultivating a welcoming environment can encourage collaboration and benefit multiple stakeholder groups. Any individual can have value to offer in a learning-oriented relationship (Figure 11.2).

The tactics to support traditionally marginalized groups can require planning and execution. A minority classification can represent membership within an identity cluster which is not in the dominant category, while

Privilege

Figure 11.2   A depiction of privilege. (Developed by Amelia Knop.)

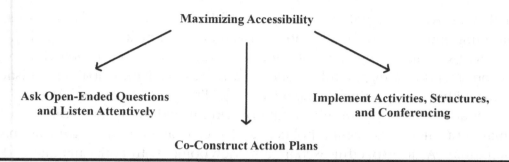

Figure 11.3   An overview of accessibility strategies. (Developed by Amelia Knop.)

vulnerable may signify individuals who can encounter risk or challenge. As a result, mentorship can co-construct resources, pathways, and best practices to ensure traditionally marginalized representatives have the possibility to achieve potential. First, privileged members should ask open-ended questions and listen attentively to gather insights about salient barriers. The relationship stage and depth can influence the specificity of guiding prompts. As a connection progresses, individuals may demonstrate higher willingness to share underlying details about resonating experiences and perceptions. Second, collaborators should co-construct action plans to resolve immediate issues within control. The ideation about possible techniques, outcomes, and implications can ignite conversations about specific next steps. As some barriers may be significant and require collective advocacy, exploration of networks can determine individuals to connect with as allies. Third, participants should implement activities, structures, and conferencing sessions with timely data collection from multimodal sources to decipher impact. The ongoing information can guide the facilitators to pivot interventions based on direct and indirect ramifications while emphasizing traditionally marginalized group-centered decision-making. A self-awareness to avoid judgment and invite feedback can strengthen the initiative components. The aptitude to use privilege for common good can extract the strengths from counterparts to encourage professional and personal growth as a mutual learning benefit (Figure 11.3).

Demonstration of Courage to Revamp Status Quo

As constructive discourse can illuminate status quo situations which require revision, program participants must convey courage to articulate and address challenges. An individual may possess confidence to ask difficult questions, share unpopular perspectives, and reinforce decision-maker accountability. However, the dissenting views should be grounded in appropriate evidence and presented in a respectful manner. If a representative exhibits unrealistic claims without supporting quantitative or qualitative data, credibility for current and subsequent insights could be diminished. Reputation can remain critical to establishing political and social capital in an organizational community. A disrespectful exchange of viewpoints with criticisms directed at people instead of salient ideas could damage a healthy workplace culture. A balanced approach is necessary with an aspirational framing so that diverse community stakeholders are motivated through a shared vision. The emphasis on compelling opportunities to generate positive impact can stimulate counterparts and broader members to initiate change. As language, modality, or dispositions can shape messaging, individuals should think carefully about content and delivery aspects. A collaborative approach of refinement can maximize the effect of activism. As a result, the courageous mindset examines existing pillars and tactfully communicates honest thoughts.

The identification of avenues to demonstrate courage can provide awareness about pathways for respectful discourse. First, requesting a meeting with decision-makers at the relevant organizational unit to express barriers and explain solutions can prompt action. The voice behaviors reaffirm a commitment to serving program members and may represent an inflection point for sense-making. Second, organizing a community collaborative inquiry session as a program administrator can facilitate dialogue through small group conversations. The willingness to accept constructive feedback and reframe challenges into learning moments can orient the next steps. Third, critiquing organizational artifacts to examine strategic and operational activities can illustrate gaps. The embedded guiding principles can manifest in a visible or invisible manner, so identifying root causes can support sense-making of current situations. An individual can assume initiative to transform the culture as a role model through behavior. The courageous activities could possess some risk as traditionally advantaged members may express frustration, impose pressure, or show resistance. A respectful discussion could minimize the chance of unhealthy conflict, but insecurity or self-interest could activate power dynamics to maintain the status quo. A courageous participant should prioritize actions that spark compelling change (Figure 11.4).

| Meeting with
Decision-Makers | Community Collaborative
Inquiry Session | Critiquing Organizational
Artifacts |

Figure 11.4 An overview of courage demonstration avenues. (Developed by Amelia Knop.)

Understanding Equity Practices in Mentorship

The equitable aspect of mentorship relationships and programs can emphasize fairness for participants. All individuals should be treated with justice, which represents interventions that are deserved. For instance, each community member warrants dignity through interactions and disseminated feedback. A counterpart should display respect for unique and dissenting views while providing honest comments with a supportive intention. Although relationship strength may differ across dyads and conflict could emerge in the developmental process, compassion for individuals should be consistently adopted. A misconception that equality and equity are synonymous can disrupt understanding of fairness in learning activities. An equal treatment of individuals can signify that actions must be uniformly implemented. In contrast, an equitable standpoint can result in differences across connections where the rationale is justified based on learner needs. For example, the number of sessions for each relationship could be identical with exactly ten meetings for an equal implementation. However, connections may have additional or fewer meetings than simultaneously conducted relationships. As individuals may have unique knowledge, skills, and experiences, the program starting point could diverge. A participant could need additional tailored support to enhance learning, while other members may desire fewer sessions in a familiar area. The care for each relationship could be generalizable, but the specific activities would differ based on strategies for impact. Through personalized interventions, the experience can generate intellectual capacity and reinforce collaboration within healthy culture.

An overview of recommendations to promote equity and address inequity can enhance the quality of learning relationships. First, implementing tailored learning activities based on articulated and recognized mentee needs can enhance value for the participant. An awareness can stem through learner self-expression and viewing of adopted behaviors. The exercises could differ in structure and execution but similarly commit to growth of the identified individual. Second, activating multimodal communication channels can ensure members process and convey insights in an understandable manner. An opportunity to use textual, visual, and auditory sources can expand sense-making to a deeper level with consideration for learning preferences. The relative engagement with each platform could be unique, but the differentiation can maximize information exchange for a participant. Third, facilitating accommodations from conversation and physical layout domains is critical to ensuring comfort. An individual may require speech-to-text software for transmission of best practices, while a counterpart could request proximity to the presenter due to hearing challenges. The accommodation type, frequency, and resources may diverge across participants, but the overarching commitment is to learning accessibility. An equitable orientation can be adopted to support any individual within the growth environment.

Understanding Diversity Practices in Mentorship

The diversity area of mentorship relationships and programs can prioritize representation from unique identities. All individuals have divergent abilities which may intersect to offer new perspectives for interpersonal learning activities. For instance, a mentor who immigrated from another country can share knowledge, skills, and experiences from specific communities. A counterpart should establish rapport so that individuals can embed visible and invisible elements within the sense-making process. Although the diverse heuristics may prompt constructive discourse, participants should interact in a respectful manner and encourage healthy conflict. A tendency may be to associate with individuals from similar identities, but connections with an assortment of community members may ignite introspection. The unique combinations of professional and personal factors can exhibit diversity across organizational units. Any views from counterparts may differ from self-identity, so engaging in open dialogue is important to understand participants at a deeper level. The diversity could be noticed both within a specific dyad and overarching initiative. For example, an older mentor could have 10 years of tenure, while a younger mentee may possess one year of experience. The age difference could possibly be determined through viewing, while the professional background would require interactional and output sources. At a program threshold, variation in ethnicities and educational qualifications could exist. However, individuals must display caution to not generate assumptions about collaborators based on identities. The labels can serve as surface-level areas, while additional insights about the specific person could explore underlying sentiments. A diverse landscape can promote differentiated best practice exchange and uncover strategies to cultivate culture.

An investigation of suggestions to naturally improve representation and leverage unique insights can spark developmental trajectories. First, identifying appropriate recruitment tactics can diversify the mentor and mentee participant pool. The activation of multimodal channels can pinpoint unique stakeholder groups, while flexible application and recommendation structures can encourage interest. The minimization of barriers can ensure accessibility for any individual to pursue participation. Second, articulating relevant selection criteria for member positions based on compelling evidence can provide opportunities for diverse identities. The analysis of existing admission metrics can determine revisions to expand the participant profiles. A co-construction process based on program goals and organizational needs can reinforce diversity incentives. Third, examining systemic bias in adopted methods through a diverse stakeholder panel can capture relevant adjustments. A consultation team with unique identities is valuable to illustrate constructive narratives for improvements in matchup allocations, initiative structures, compiled resources, and session facilitators. An authentic aptitude to embrace diversity can be mobilized to integrate unique individuals and viewpoints for effectiveness in decision-making.

Understanding Inclusivity Practices in Mentorship

The inclusivity element of mentorship relationships and programs can focus on enhanced belongingness for stakeholders. The perceived acceptance within a dyad or learning community could influence the ability to maximize collective potential. For instance, a mentee who feels invited to participate in learning conversations may demonstrate improved engagement and motivation to share perspectives. The development of inclusive contexts can require time and effort as participants collaboratively establish norms. A viewpoint about belongingness can evolve based on textual, visual, and auditory sources as individuals synthesize data to engage in sense-making. Although representation may be diverse, inclusivity is not guaranteed within a mentorship intervention. The authentic devotion to creating welcoming environments depends on purposeful and consistent action. If individuals demonstrate volatility through dispositions and behaviors in activities, their counterparts may encounter ambiguity, which can influence the discernment process. An inclusive landscape could simultaneously enact an exclusive context due to boundary conditions, but a mentorship initiative should ensure belongingness for learners. For example, a cultivated peer relationship may involve a mentor and mentee with similar professional backgrounds. As a result, individuals with divergent backgrounds may be excluded from the dialogue. The exclusive nature could limit diverse perspectives, so members must think about how to eliminate barriers to involve broader stakeholders within the program. An inclusive domain can encourage ideation and reaffirm the importance of ongoing collaborative efforts.

A synthesis of possibilities to generate belongingness and establish environments of psychological safety can foster learning. First, articulating norms about voice behaviors can provide opportunities for all participants to share unique perspectives. The dominance in a mentorship conversation can discourage individuals from presenting insights. A co-constructed structure to permit expression is valuable to spark brainstorming and constructive dialogue. The lack of explicit norms may prompt implicit processes to transpire, while conversation imbalance and power dynamics could emerge. Second, rotating the facilitator and learner roles can invite participants to mobilize diverse developmental strategies. The flexible nature of relationship activities can empower individuals to consider unique perspectives and expand the toolkit of actionable approaches. A pivoted implementation for responsibilities can reinforce bidirectional exchange, which may be conducive to perceptions of inclusion. Third, launching professional learning communities to supplement mentorship can empower individuals to disseminate ideas across contexts. Although a productive and supportive relationship is compelling, integration within the broader program and organizational unit is helpful for generalizable belongingness. A multitude of positive formal and informal connections can prompt individuals to navigate issues with supporting mechanisms. As inclusivity is an ongoing activity that requires an iterative cycle of planning, execution, and reflection, understanding about phenomena is critical to adaptation (Figure 11.5).

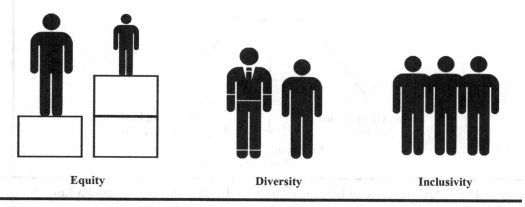

Figure 11.5   A depiction of equity, diversity, and inclusivity. (Developed by Amelia Knop.)

Bias Identification and Awareness Tool Adoption

The awareness about individual or collective bias can guide program administrators about strategies to maximize learning facilitation. An area of bias may represent a tendency to view an individual or situation in a specific manner. For instance, an experienced educator may serve as a mentor for a novice teacher and assume that the mentee has limited knowledge to be successful. If the viewpoint is explicitly communicated or implicitly inferred, the suggested scenario may emerge as a self-fulfilling prophecy. The conveyed bias can accentuate subjectivity throughout learning activities, which can limit the openness needed to authentically engage in the growth process. The perceptions can manifest as taken-for-granted assumptions since thoughts may be reinforced repeatedly over time through complementary sources. A mentorship relationship and program can provide a meaningful platform for individuals to improve awareness about any exhibited tendencies. As bias can occur in activity design, conferencing sessions, and progress reviews, a critical analysis can motivate individuals to think from comprehensive standpoints.

The depiction of awareness tools can offer strategies for implementation in mentorship initiatives. First, asking open-ended questions in a comfortable environment can motivate the respondents to honestly express their sentiments. The follow-up prompts can encourage members to expand on provided answers and explain the significance or implications of themes. A higher-level thinking process can equip individuals with the

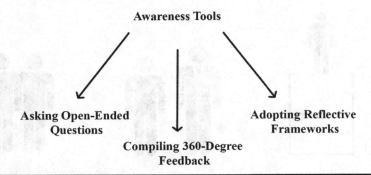

Figure 11.6   An overview of bias awareness tools. (Developed by Amelia Knop.)

capacity to more effectively pinpoint bias at the moment. Second, compiling 360-degree feedback about task and relationship activities can share insights from diverse levels. The illustrated views can posit considerations for participants, while deviation between self and unique stakeholder feedback may ignite introspection. An exchange of perspectives can assist with the development of professional and personal action plans. Third, adopting reflective frameworks can orient individuals to think purposefully about common biases within the organization. A start, continue, and stop method can provide a format for ongoing improvement, while co-construction of institutional models can offer strategies. The generally framed techniques can be tailored specifically to the contextual trends and needs (Figure 11.6).

Consolidation of Equity, Diversity, and Inclusivity in Mentorship

A devotion to maximizing accessibility in the mentorship process is central to developing intellectual capacity and healthy workplace culture. The attention to personal privilege can guide individuals to address barriers for improved achievement of traditionally marginalized groups. A willingness to display courage can empower participants to improve fairness, representation, and belongingness in programs. Although biases may exist, critical evaluation can identify relevant adaptations. An accessibility objective remains critical across all roles in a mentorship pathway.

Chapter 12

Transitioning from Mentee to Mentor to Program Leader

A mentorship program can empower individuals to embark on a lifelong learning journey through ongoing best practice exchange with diverse collaborators. The commitment to fairness, representation, and belongingness can cultivate a positive developmental experience from both intellectual capacity and healthy workplace culture domains. As mentorship activities can align with the professional and personal identity, participants may perceive the opportunity to be a vocational endeavor. This chapter captures a possible mentorship pathway for individuals to consistently facilitate learning for themselves and their community counterparts. Although a learning journey may be perceived as linear, the process can be iterative and personalized with unique progression between stages. The pivot between roles can transpire over time, while participants may adopt a single role in a relationship and multiple positions within a broader program. A devotion to learner-centered activities can spark a visible or invisible legacy across diverse organizational units. As individuals interpret value from engagement in the initiative, motivation to sustain participation from formal or informal standpoints could grow. A review of anticipatory, call-to-action, and synthesis stages within a discernment process can influence action plans for transitioning to unfamiliar roles. The co-construction of an authentic mentorship ecosystem can encourage connectivity of individuals for the foreseeable future. An explicit articulation of learning possibilities can ignite awareness about engagement opportunities, while pursuit of mentee, mentor, and program leader roles can synthesize insights about unique positionalities.

DOI: 10.4324/9781032715247-13

The guiding questions can challenge organizations to think beyond a relationship level to create enriching learning conditions at a program threshold. First, individuals should consider: How is the mentorship pathway envisioned holistically in an organization, and why? A pathway motivates learners to proceed in diverse trajectories based on needs, interests, and preferences. A precise understanding of program objectives based on quantitative and qualitative evidence is critical to establishing a shared vision. The implications of connections can collectively influence organizational activities from strategic and operational areas. If a pathway has termination points with no subsequent opportunities, individuals may exit the mentorship community shortly after a formal end date is surpassed. However, a program can reframe termination stages into transition phases so that individuals can continue growth as lifelong learners. Purposeful ideation about initiative links may depend on organizational size, resources, aspirations, and structures. Second, practitioners should consider: How can participants assume multiple roles concurrently, and why? A compartmentalized framing may position individuals in a single relationship at a time, where the participant is either a mentor or mentee. However, an interconnected lens could invite members to simultaneously pursue multiple roles. An individual could serve as a mentor within a first relationship while engaging as a mentee within a second relationship. The additional connections can provide complementary opportunities for learning as individuals can exchange best practices in multiple contexts. Although the relationship network may become intertwined, the organized chaos can create novel growth moments due to learning associations. As a result, a willingness to attempt and revise strategies based on diverse data can promote improvement.

Non-Linear Mentorship Pathway

The investigation of positionalities within the mentorship pathway can illuminate the strategies for direct participation. The direct link signifies that individuals can be involved in co-construction processes for activities, while the indirect connection represents individuals who are impacted in the broader community. First, the identified mentee participates in a developmental journey with opportunities to accumulate novel knowledge, skills, and experiences. The mentee identities could originate from a wide range as individuals may engage in peer and traditional programs. Although a mentee is viewed as a learner, the participant has opportunities to impart best practices to the mentor collaborator. Second, the designated mentor facilitates development for counterparts with process orientation, non-evaluative feedback, and learner-centered activities. A mentor could be selected for a relationship based on content or delivery abilities, as significant knowledge within a specialized discipline may not be necessary depending on program goals. The mentor has an ongoing responsibility to evoke an exchange of insights through adopted styles and interventions. A facilitator should recognize the bidirectional nature of information flow since the title does not represent imposition. Third, a program leader is responsible for planning, executing, and advising so participants achieve identified goals. The individual is a higher-level facilitator or administrator while collaborating as needed with dyads to offer tailored support.

Although a mentorship stakeholder may perceive that individuals transition sequentially between the mentee, mentor, and leader roles, an iterative progression could transpire. A non-linear pivot may occur where participants proceed in a unique pathway, while members could simultaneously assume multiple positions. An individual may become a mentee as an entry point in a mentorship trajectory to learn about activities from an empirical lens, which could equip the member to embark on future mentor opportunities. However, an organization could initially allocate an individual to a mentor position based on relevant characteristics or provide a mentee assignment to build capacity after previously serving as a mentor. A program leader could possess mentee and mentor experiences, but an institution may assign the candidate to the administrative role based on professional role responsibilities without prior involvement. For instance, a human resources manager could be linked to the initiative in a project portfolio. An individual could be a mentee and mentor in multiple relationships or serve as a mentor and leader concurrently. As a result, possibilities should be considered based on individualized profiles.

Mentorship Program Legacy and Future Involvement

A comprehensive mentorship program has the possibility to cultivate a positive legacy within the identified organization or local environment. The legacy can represent the extent of impact from implemented activities where the implications may be transformative and retained for a longer timeframe. As individuals will exhibit diverse positionalities and identities, the relative perception of program legacy could vary from positive or negative standpoints. For example, a manager may appreciate a mentorship initiative as the supervised team could offer enhanced insights into deliverables. However, individuals may express ongoing frustration with a management team if participation in a mentorship relationship is required and interpreted value is low. A positive legacy could be critical to motivate prospective members for the program while expanding the best practice exchange forum from the formal to informal landscape. The individuals may not initially recognize the benefits of engagement, so effective mentorship conferences can uncover resonating experiences in an explicit manner for ongoing application.

An exploration of techniques to generate awareness about program legacy could guide implementation within an organization. First, highlighting success stories can permit individuals to share compelling narratives in an authentic manner. The activation of multimodal channels can distribute the sentiments to diverse stakeholders. The presented viewpoints can mobilize best practices throughout a community and showcase engagement benefits. Second, pinpointing salient intrinsic motivators for participants can influence facilitators to focus on how to create personalized meaning. A purposeful mentorship program based on co-constructed learning priorities can encourage individuals to disseminate positive perspectives. The aspirations and philosophies for participation can diverge, so uniform implementation of learning principles may not achieve the highest possible impact level. Third, consistently compiling quantitative and qualitative evidence can capture metrics and themes. The accumulated details can inform program collaborators about the established impact while offering suggestions to enhance decision-making strategies. The diversified sources can guide conferencing sessions and denote success factors for relationships. Fourth, acknowledging challenges and conveying commitment to improvement can reaffirm the aspirational framing. A willingness to adapt based on expressed perspectives can exhibit how the organization values collaborators. A program is not expected to be perfect, but disingenuously showing positive areas only can be viewed with lower credibility (Figure 12.1).

As individuals may express motivation to continue involvement in mentorship activities for future iterations, administrators should think creatively about how to permit engagement. First, program graduates could have formal opportunities to participate in alternative positions for an expanded professional and personal learning portfolio. A mentee may be invited to serve as a mentor in a subsequent initiative or assist with program administration based on displayed abilities. The past program experiences can offer valuable insights to consider for improved interventions. Second,

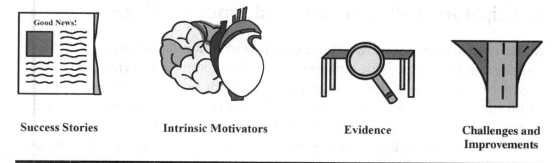

Figure 12.1   An overview of legacy awareness techniques. (Developed by Amelia Knop.)

informal involvement of past participants through guest speaker sessions or coffee chat discussions can permit bidirectional exchange. An individual could facilitate an in-person or virtual workshop as a tailored developmental opportunity for current program members. The personalized conversation possibility invites individuals to share perspectives and questions, while matchups can be established through booking webpages or outreach. Third, identifying platforms for professional learning communities can encourage members to connect with counterparts following a relationship or program. An optional alumnus gathering can invite collaborators to offer progress updates, pinpoint applicable resources, or discuss solutions to emergent challenges. The available channels can permit individuals to sustain contact as needed. To foster a positive legacy, programs can specify pathways for ongoing community involvement (Figure 12.2).

Figure 12.2   An overview of future involvement activities. (Developed by Amelia Knop.)

Anticipatory, Call-to-Action, and Synthesis Stages

As individuals proceed toward the conclusion of a relationship, transitioning sessions with anticipatory, call-to-action, and synthesis stages can depict possible next steps. To embark on a new relationship or program, individuals should reconsider learning goals, aspirations, and needs. The transition conference could involve a mentor, administrator, or supervisor depending on the current mentee, mentor, or administrator position, respectively. The session could occur before or after the formalized program end date, but participants are encouraged to identify timing based on personal readiness. The intention is to spark reflection with consideration of retrospective and prospective pathways. First, the anticipatory stage motivates participants to brainstorm possibilities for future development without ideation constraints. The process could start with an independent reflection about strengths and improvement areas, where evidence and perspectives are recorded for future reference. A conferencing session could be organized for the individual to review progress based on initial co-constructed objectives. As a mentorship program is not evaluative, the purpose is to articulate the expected implications with rationale. Active engagement in the introspection activities can organize best practices cognitively as limitless learning may have occurred for the participants. An aptitude to transform implicit perspectives into an explicit format can empower collaborators to leverage insights in future endeavors. The anticipatory phase provokes salient insights from a learning intervention.

Second, the call-to-action stage encourages individuals to adopt best practices in an immediate manner so that goals in new and existing areas can be developed. A call represents an invitation for individuals to implement novel learning to enhance task and relationship activities. The vocational sense evokes metacognition about how the insights converge or diverge with the individualized identity. The convergence can reinforce internalized practices and be leveraged to extend impact, while the divergence may prompt reconsideration of existing activities. Although an individual may believe that growth only transpires when changes are implemented, a deeper appreciation of personal purpose can clarify the appropriateness of current strategies. As a result, positive reinforcement of present behaviors with compelling justification can spark awareness about implementation ramifications. A transition meeting can pinpoint relevant intellectual, financial, human, physical, and technological resources which may be critical for integration of lessons learned. The specification of action steps can narrow the assembled information from the anticipatory stage to focus time and effort on meaningful initiatives. A recalibration for the future learning orientation can generate understanding about the needs to accumulate novel competencies.

Third, the synthesis stage seeks to consolidate the resonating best practices and identify the forthcoming mentorship community activities. As the anticipatory phase sparks ideation and call to action emphasizes practical implementation, the synthesis captures the next mentorship journey. For instance, a mentor who has shared best practices about educational pedagogy may have received questions from a mentee about effective technological platforms. The mentor could have subsequently pinpointed a need to expand technological understanding through the transition session phases. As a result, the mentor could participate in an upcoming program as a mentee to learn from a counterpart who has knowledge, skills, and experiences in the realm of technology. A synthesis activity could illuminate formal mentorship opportunities within the organization or informal possibilities through participation in the broader community. The conferencing strategy could be adopted with the relationship counterpart in the closing exercises to explore mutual interest in continuation of the connection. A purposeful analysis of the next steps can consistently prompt participants to think about diverse professional and personal learning opportunities. The dialogue can encourage reflection with tailored prompts from collaborators (Figure 12.3).

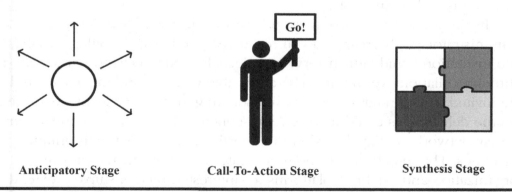

| Anticipatory Stage | Call-To-Action Stage | Synthesis Stage |

Figure 12.3 An overview of transitioning session stages. (Developed by Amelia Knop.)

Maintaining Relationship Connectivity

Although a mentorship collaboration may formally conclude at an established timeframe, strategies for connectivity could be initiated from within the relation or facilitated through the program. A relationship should be extended if both participants perceive authentic value from the exchange, which could occur from task or relationship domains. The productive and supportive elements can maximize the possibility for sustained success in an ongoing learning intervention. An assortment of strategies for connectivity may be leveraged from relationship participants. First, periodic check-in meetings could be planned for progress updates from professional and personal areas. The session timing should be co-constructed based on relationship factors, but a quarterly interaction could be a baseline for scheduling. The discussions could highlight how the lessons learned have impacted activities and pose open-ended questions to delve deeper into emerging developmental priorities. Second, visits could be organized where a participant shadows the counterpart or seeks feedback about current projects. The live sessions could occur as needed with outreach from the relevant learner, while formative insights could be posited to process a new perspective. The focus could be on task completion or performance where the viewing, interaction, and output sources provide evidence for thoughtful discussion. Third, attendance at practitioner conferences could permit members to reconnect. The relationship themes could motivate individuals to register for a learning opportunity in a similar growth area. The formal sessions could be complemented with informal development through experiences. As learning can occur in any context, diversified opportunities may be pursued based on interests.

The suggestion of connectivity pathways could stem from program administrators with organizational resources to encourage dialogue. First, the institution could launch service projects for individuals to participate through collaborative inquiry. The applicable mentors and mentees could be invited to the initiative based on resonating areas of collective expertise. As the deliverables could involve representatives from diverse connections, a new network may evolve where the participants interact with unique identities. The intention is to both generate new best practices for the organization and establish platforms for interested relationships to extend the momentum. Second, the organization could host optional professional development workshops based on the salient needs expressed in the

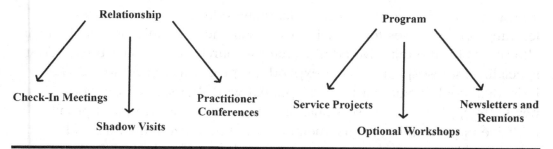

Figure 12.4 An overview of connectivity strategies. (Developed by Amelia Knop.)

closing survey. The mentor and mentee could receive resource stipends to reduce barriers to participation, while the activity could be tailored to the conveyed growth priorities. A strategic timing could occur a few weeks or months after the program to offer opportunities for individuals to reflect on best practices. The collaborators could be invited to facilitate future workshops to share insights across organizational units. Third, cohort newsletters and reunion gatherings can be implemented to voluntarily reconnect members. The newsletter could highlight achievements of participants in the aftermath of an initiative to show the benefits of involvement. The reunion could occur annually or bi-annually as an avenue for individuals to offer insights about experiences, aspirations, and milestones. A multimodal approach is valuable so that individuals can participate in a manner that aligns with personalized preferences. A stakeholder consultation could illuminate additional techniques for connectivity (Figure 12.4).

Opportunities for Indirect Engagement in a Mentorship Community

An overview of opportunities within a mentorship environment can diversify possibilities for engagement so that individuals may indirectly generate positive impact. As a mentor, mentee, or administrator journey could cultivate attachment to a program, former participants may communicate interest in support activities. If an individual is not available or interested in being directly involved in the initiative, indirect pathways could be activated. The members could contribute to participant learning from an external standpoint through unique interventions. First, individuals could support a program by offering resources which may reduce barriers or extend learning opportunities for participants. A stakeholder could provide financial allocations for the initiative administrator to purchase infrastructure, recruit specialized guest speakers, and expand the program support team. The individual could volunteer to host optional workshops, author cohort newsletters, plan reunion sessions, offer logistical assistance, and promote initiative opportunities. A past member could mobilize hardware and software elements for the program team such as technological devices, equipment, or learning system access. The willingness to integrate diverse resources can ensure richness in adopted activities while improving ability of administrators to facilitate tailored learning interventions for newly selected participants. A dialogue with initiative decision-makers can illustrate needs and guide individuals to identify resonating resources for maximum return on community investment.

Second, individuals could impart service to the program as part of an advisory team which guides the strategic orientation. The participation of collaborators from diverse visible and invisible identities can encourage constructive discourse about approaches to improve the initiative quality. A review of overarching organizational objectives may illuminate necessary revisions based on compiled data sources. The recommendations could influence operational techniques which would be applied through the program administrator team. Although a panel could function similarly to a board of directors, the distinction is that the administrators do not report to the advisory team. The advisors are involved to offer best practices for consideration and spark ideation through perspective-taking, but the administrator autonomy mitigates power dynamics which could possibly pivot the focus from learners. As individuals would have previously participated in the mentorship initiative, the personalized experiences could offer themes for deliberation in planning sessions. The investigated strategies for effective mentorship should be adopted so the advisory team can facilitate best practice exchange to enhance the program. A sense of responsibility to generate impact could motivate authentic expression.

Third, individuals could become mentorship program ambassadors to encourage participation from organizational community members. The representatives could highlight benefits of engagement in mentorship through formal and informal opportunities. For example, a supervisor could explain how mentorship is a valuable experience to new team members at a project meeting or through individualized conversations.

| Offering Resources | Advisory Team | Program Ambassadors |

Figure 12.5 An overview of indirect engagement opportunities. (Developed by Amelia Knop.)

The ambassadors can motivate contacts within the institution to apply for mentee, mentor, or program leader roles. An invitation to participate could represent an inflection point where a stakeholder is empowered to pursue a novel learning opportunity. The representatives could offer recommendations to the program selection team for consideration, especially in larger organizations where the participant pool could be significant and scarce resources exist. However, administrators should retain awareness that referrals could stem from similarity. As a result, suggestions from ambassadors should not represent the only source within a screening process and instead complement available data avenues. As champions for the program, the alumni could cultivate a contagious learning environment where many individuals may aspire to embark on a novel mentorship journey (Figure 12.5).

Mentorship Role Interconnection and Rotation

As a mentorship program can require engagement from mentees, mentors, and initiative leaders to improve success, the roles are interconnected in a learning intervention. The clear identification of responsibilities can collectively generate positive outcomes and minimize possible challenges. The co-construction of norms could involve an analysis of information flow between the relationship and institution. A synergistic alignment of mentorship organizational units can expand best practice exchange avenues and leverage untapped resources. A mentorship intervention involves multilevel considerations, so intellectual capacity can grow through a collaborative learning orientation. The motivation to share insights in a bidirectional manner for an ongoing timeframe naturally encourages respect

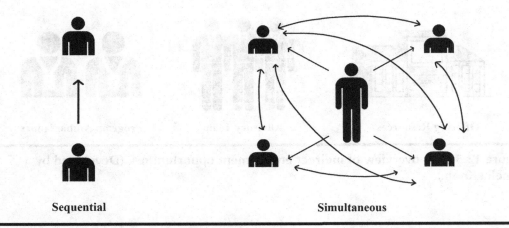

Sequential   Simultaneous

Figure 12.6   An overview of role rotation structures. (Developed by Amelia Knop.)

as a signal of healthy workplace culture. As individuals could adopt multiple roles within a program, the positionalities should instead be viewed as identity elements. A self-awareness about mentee, mentor, and administrator identities could foster learning, facilitative, and supportive behaviors which can benefit any context.

The rotation of roles within a mentorship program can encourage individuals to assume diverse perspectives and engage in deeper sense-making about learning strategies. First, an initiative design could permit individuals to participate in one relationship as a mentor and another connection as a mentee at the same time. An opportunity to engage in development with both facilitator and learner identities can ignite reflection about how to maximize growth. Second, a sequential structure could assign an individual to a mentee role for an initial segment with an opportunity to transition into a mentor role for the following section. The next program cycle could admit mentees, while the most recent mentee cohort may serve as the new mentor pool. The intention is to encourage timely application of learning skills based on experience and motivate individuals to participate authentically in the journey through unique positions (Figure 12.6).

Consolidation of Transitioning from Mentee to Mentor to Program Leader

A reframed view of the mentorship pathway illustrates that individuals can move between positions over time based on non-linear developmental needs.

The opportunity to engage in a growth network can permit members to assume roles concurrently as facilitators and learners. The commitment to creating a positive legacy can guide decision-making, while involvement in anticipatory, call-to-action, and synthesis stages can shape the next steps. As program alumni can be reintegrated into mentorship, the activities may represent cyclical and everlasting phenomena.

Conclusion: Synthesis of Lessons Learned

Through an investigation of diverse mentorship themes, practitioners have an opportunity to engage in introspection about existing and anticipated activities in organizational contexts. Although numerous considerations or best practices have been conveyed, mentorship depends on learner-centered relationships and requires alignment of interventions with needs. As a result, the general recommendations must be tailored to the specific developmental landscape to maximize value for participants. An aptitude to compile quantitative and qualitative data with viewing, interaction, or output sources can illuminate insights for decision-making. A collective effort is necessary to consistently improve mentorship interventions, as novel perspectives can suggest adaptations. Mentorship is represented as a bidirectional learning relationship with best practice exchange between organizational units to achieve collaboratively identified goals. The two-way information flow reinforces that mentors are facilitators in the growth journey, while mentees can similarly prompt development for the mentor counterpart. The collaborative emphasis exhibits the importance of allocating time early in the connection to establishing norms and generating rapport. Every mentorship relationship and program can create a differentiated identity, which can influence activities, conferences, and self-assessment processes. A relationship should align with an overarching program in two critical domains. First, mentorship should motivate the participants to build intellectual capacity with new knowledge, skills, and experiences. Second, mentorship should help cultivate a healthy workplace culture of respect and

DOI: 10.4324/9781032715247-14

Intellectual Capacity   **Healthy Workplace Culture**

Figure 13.1   An overview of overarching mentorship areas. (Developed by Amelia Knop.)

support. As a result, the examined areas should equip administrators to initiate or revamp mentorship initiatives (Figure 13.1).

As each chapter posits two guiding questions to encourage critical and creative thinking about the learning objectives, the conclusion will revisit the expressed prompts. An explanation of sample resonating best practices can consolidate lessons learned and spark novel reflection. The inquiry topics were framed as open-ended questions to invite articulation of diverse narratives. A review of guiding questions with mentorship program stakeholders could provide a lens for assessing initiative progress. As insights are accumulated through exposure to diverse concepts, respectful, constructive discourse is valuable to enhance sense-making. A willingness to explore unique perspectives is integral so that mentees, mentors, and administrators can build a positive learning environment. The illustrated analysis of guiding questions suggests possible interpretations from the author, but both agreement and disagreement are welcomed. Positive reinforcement is meaningful to evoke awareness about processes which may be implemented in a subconscious manner. Meanwhile, the motivation to challenge, refine, and extend viewpoints can demonstrate new possibilities for adaptation in a mentorship intervention. As a result, the offered synthesis can signify a starting point for individuals to assemble and apply strategies throughout a practical environment. The aspiration is for organizational community members to increase competence to implement mentorship activities with confidence and pivot based on outcomes (Figure 13.2).

Competence   Confidence

Figure 13.2   A depiction of competence and confidence. (Developed by Amelia Knop.)

Chapter 1: Mentorship Defined

As mentorship may be interpreted uniquely based on organizational factors or member heuristics, a shared and explicit understanding is necessary from the outset. First, practitioners should reconsider: How does the organization define mentorship, and why? The differentiation of mentorship from alternative constructs conveys common elements as process-oriented, facilitative, practical, non-evaluative, and learner-centered. Second, stakeholders should rethink: How has the conceptualization of mentorship changed over time for diverse stakeholders, and why? The opportunities for peer or traditional relationships, formal or informal structures, and team or individual involvement can impact implementation. A review of interaction frequency, relationship length, and interaction modality may evolve based on emergent program needs.

Chapter 2: Participant Identities and Responsibilities

An attention to individual factors can provide details to process diverse viewpoints, while clear articulation of relationship tasks can convey expected actions for the collaborators. The mentorship environment may offer a blend of educational opportunities and lived experiences to pursue expressed goals. First, practitioners should reconsider: What identities are necessary to enhance intellectual capacity and healthy workplace culture, and why? A mentor should examine communication, active listening, and critical or creative thinking skills to effectively facilitate learning for a counterpart. In relation, a mentee should exhibit adaptability, problem-solving, and collaboration skills to authentically engage in growth exchanges. Second, stakeholders should rethink: What are the common dynamic or static responsibilities of mentors and mentees within a two-way learning relationship, and why? The actions involve initiation, planning, and assessment or reporting areas, which benefit from co-construction based on learning goals or strengths. As a connection evolves, new activities may emerge, so members must explicitly denote allocations.

Chapter 3: Signals to Start Mentorship Programs

The catalyst to initiate or revise mentorship programs could stem from visible and invisible indicators in the organizational ecosystem. A focus on surface-level factors only can neglect the underlying and possibly more significant phenomena. First, practitioners should reconsider: How does the organization use data collection techniques to identify signals for mentorship program initiation, and why? A blended approach with viewing, interactional, and output sources can provide multimodal avenues, while quantitative and qualitative elements can enrichen the analysis. Second, stakeholders should rethink: How can a program achieve specified performance indicators with diverse constraints, and why? A purposeful recruitment and training strategy can enact a shared vision, while leveraging intangible resources can navigate constraints.

Chapter 4: Outcomes for Mentees, Mentors, and Communities

Through examination about possible results in mentorship relationships or programs, participants can recognize the positive, negative, neutral, and ambivalent consequences. First, practitioners should reconsider: How can organizations navigate any complexities effectively, and why? The diverse organizational units may encounter trade-offs, so individual, team, institution, and community benefits could prompt drawbacks for counterparts. As a result, mitigation plans can include interest statements, clear expectations, matchup strategy, training modules, multimodal data collection, and former member presentations. Second, stakeholders should rethink: What benefits could spark mentee participation, and why? A compelling benefit requires alignment with the mentee developmental zone. The opportunity to compile novel best practices, improve self-belief, and achieve meaningful goals could incentivize participation. An honest acknowledgment of challenges can ensure individuals are prepared for the experience.

Chapter 5: Mentorship Styles and Philosophies

An enhanced comprehension of mentorship approaches can motivate participants to adopt appropriate strategies for maximum positive impact. First, practitioners should reconsider: How can the development of a philosophy generate shared understanding, and why? A personalized philosophy can illustrate resonating needs, interests, and preferences. The explicit awareness about critical elements, social causes, and decision-making priorities can formulate self-identity through honest articulation. Second, stakeholders should rethink: What mentorship styles or blends resonate with a particular philosophy, and why? A selected style manifests guiding beliefs through dispositions, so purposeful behaviors can enact relevant learning. The transformational style includes questioning innovator, quiet role model, or perspective taker identities, while the transactional style involves goal setter, reward distributor, or diligent organizer identities.

Chapter 6: Building Relationships and Establishing Norms

As mentorship connections have the potential to generate lifelong learning, extra attention to developing rapport and co-constructing norms is essential in the initiation stage. The perceived delay with extra time and effort to learn about the counterpart could accelerate growth in subsequent phases. First, practitioners should reconsider: What norms and objectives are important for organizational mentorship initiatives, and why? A productive framing may specify progress metrics, weighting goals, time parameters, and constructive discourse. A supportive lens can clarify encouragement, strength orientation, attentive listening, and well-being activities. Second, stakeholders should rethink: How can knowledge about counterpart participant identities enhance relationship building, and why? The expression of learning styles and intelligences can respectively indicate compelling sense-making techniques or distinguishing competencies. An appreciation of individual factors can provide insight to tailor interventions to a specific context.

Chapter 7: Before, During, and After Mentorship

The non-linear mentorship journey includes many activities to spark development, so introspection about initial, ongoing, and concluding stages can guide implementation. First, practitioners should reconsider: What milestones display participant progress in a mentorship relationship, and why? The identification of objectives, matchup factors, resources, and data collection avenues can occur at initiation, while experiences, discussions, questions, showcases, or portfolios may transpire on an ongoing basis. A conclusion can specify successes, challenges, and next steps, while fostering transition into informal relations. Second, stakeholders should rethink: What activities are needed for the specific learner at each stage, and why? The advisory, encouragement, asking, and challenger approaches could be adopted based on the developmental phase. As a relationship strengthens, constructive discourse and deeper questions may emerge.

Chapter 8: Verbal and Written Feedback

Although communication of positive and constructive feedback may appear simplistic in a relationship, individuals must think strategically about diverse factors to align intention with impact. First, practitioners should reconsider: What strategies or structures are necessary to offer meaningful feedback, and why? An appropriate feedback platform should be mobilized based on the sensitivity or complexity of message content and delivery. The feedback should be delicate, thoughtful, aspirational, and practical, while individuals should have relevant processing space. A directive mentor-initiated or facilitative mentee-driven strategy could depend on learning objectives. Second, stakeholders should rethink: What are organizational priorities for feedback type, and why? An awareness about program expectations can influence linguistics, conversation atmosphere, and body language, while navigation of conflicts requires a compassionate lens. A standardized or individualized style may influence perceived equity, timeliness, and consistency.

Chapter 9: Improve Engagement with Effective Questions

To encourage genuine engagement within a learning conversation, counterparts must identify compelling questioning techniques. First, practitioners should reconsider: How can questioning spark discussions about deeper situations, and why? An individual should view an effective prompt as an opportunity to pursue growth through metacognition. An open-ended inquiry could invite underlying narratives to spark sense-making, while closed-ended questions could categorize responses for common apprehension. Second, stakeholders should rethink: How can content and style enhance receptivity to reflection, and why? The language conventions, timing, sequencing, and follow-up opportunities could be explored to broaden entry points for maintained dialogue. A variation in implemented styles can synthesize expressed perspectives, spark developmental trajectories, and pinpoint learning gaps to convey tailored resources.

Chapter 10: Self-Assessment Scorecard

The development of a tailored framework to capture progress can guide action plans, identify formative milestones, and align learning interventions. A scorecard resource can specify criteria, weightings, activities, resources, timeframes, and success indicators for participants. First, practitioners should reconsider: How can a balanced scorecard incentivize authentic learning and appropriate risk-taking, and why? A standard based approach with below, meet, and exceed categories could mitigate stress relative to percentage scores. The intention is to spark engagement and innovation, while evidence is compiled to inform the next steps. Second, stakeholders should rethink: What organization-specific categories should be included within the scorecard, and why? The general themes may involve intellectual capacity, relationship building, participant self-efficacy, new perspective synthesis, and additional responsibility preparedness. A criterion could be replaced depending on the relationship and program developmental intentions.

Chapter 11: Equity, Diversity, and Inclusivity in Mentorship

An environment that prioritizes accessibility can offer limitless possibilities for mentorship participants to pursue individualized potential. First, practitioners should reconsider: What organizational equity, diversity, and inclusivity challenges limit mentorship effectiveness, and why? The differentiated opportunities, multimodal communications, or accommodations can improve fairness, while appropriate recruitment, relevant criteria, and examined bias may expand representation. A commitment to voice behaviors, rotational roles, and growth communities can offer belongingness. Second, stakeholders should rethink: How can relationships with unique identities generate unprecedented learning, and why? As individuals possess diverse visible and invisible elements, leveraging privilege to support marginalized groups can ignite change. An increased awareness about bias can occur through constructive discourse in unique relationships.

Chapter 12: Transitioning from Mentee to Mentor to Program Leader

As individuals have diverse aspirations and identities, an examination of the non-linear mentorship trajectory can illustrate possibilities for continued involvement. First, practitioners should reconsider: How is the mentorship pathway envisioned holistically in an organization, and why? The direct participation impacts learners, so mentees, mentors, and administrators are integrated to facilitate the exchange of best practices. The indirect engagement could occur through broader community representatives as resource donors, advisory team members, or program ambassadors. As individuals could enter the pathway through diverse positionalities, creativity about strategies to build community is valuable. Second, stakeholders should rethink: How can participants assume multiple roles concurrently, and why? A member could be involved as a mentor and mentee through simultaneous relationships to encourage perspective-taking. The mentorship identity could be assumed formally or informally, so organizations could establish environments for ongoing development to empower any individual in pursuit of potential.

Consolidation of Best Practices and Next Steps in Journey

The opportunity to revisit guiding questions about mentorship topics can motivate individuals to pinpoint changes in lessons learned. A mentorship relationship or program is consistently evolving, which aligns with development as a dynamic construct. As a cognitive reconstruction may occur through authentic engagement in mentorship initiatives, significant growth can emerge when practitioners retain openness to diverse perspectives. An enriching mentorship adventure may stimulate, challenge, and inspire individuals to implement new knowledge, skills, or experiences in organizational activities. The inflection point can transpire spontaneously for mentors and mentees, so willingness to exhibit effort in the learning dialogue can spark transformative implications. A compelling environment investigates success factors at a deeper level with a consistent interest in improvement. As a result, the illustrated topics provide best practices for practitioners to synthesize across organizational units through interventions.

Although individuals, teams, institutions, or organizations may consistently change, mentorship could remain as a compelling and commonplace strategy to generate growth. A single question was conveyed at the outset: How can the initiation, adaptation, or extension of mentorship practices improve organizational task and relationship behaviors for program participants? The launch of purposeful two-way learning initiatives can amplify existing efforts in professional and personal development. An aptitude to revise approaches using accumulated evidence can maximize accessibility for individuals from diverse identities. Through expanded program activities, the breadth and depth of salient implications could transcend expectations. Involvement in a mentorship community has the possibility to impact countless stakeholders with unprecedented results. Welcome again to the wonderful world of organizational mentorship (Figure 13.3).

Welcome to the wonderful world of organizational mentorship!

Figure 13.3 A depiction of limitless learning possibilities. (Developed by Amelia Knop.)

Index

Printed in the United States
by Baker & Taylor Publisher Services